ESSENTIAL *take care* TIPS

A Practical Guide to Self-Care

Enhanced with Essential Oils

Jennifer Antkowiak

Some of the material in this book, ESSENTIAL TAKE CARE TIPS, originally appeared in TAKE CARE TIPS published by St. Lynn's Press in 2009

www.TakeCareTips.com

To those I am blessed to care for,

and for all of you who make

the time to care for those you love.

SYMBOL KEY

Denotes number of drops
of Essential Oil to add.

Oil Blend

Diffuser Blend

Bodycare Recipe

Rollerball Blend

Food Recipe

Spray Recipe

Contents

As a special heart-felt gift for you as you begin your journey to better self-care, I want to share something that will help you ease into the right mindset for this important work.

Throughout this book, I invite you (and show you how) to be more gentle with yourself. Being able to do that effectively, goes along with a need to heal the heart. Often times, we carry around feelings of blame, guilt, regret, and other deep emotions that make our hearts feel heavy, and block our joy. We need to develop a routine of "blessing and releasing" to clear the distractions, discover and align with our true purpose, and re-connect with our own desires. I'm sharing this book with the intent of helping you find your way back to feelings of true health, happiness, and hope.

With this in mind I've created a signature Essential Oil Blend that I hope you will make and wear knowing that you are wrapped in love and appreciation. Think of it as a heavenly hug, filling you with the comfort that you are not alone, and that everything's going to be alright.

If you are new to Essential Oils, I look forward to teaching you about what they are, and how to safely use them to support your physical and emotional health. I have lots of information about that for you at www.TakeCareTips.com as well. For now, though, here is The White Feather Blend...

WHITE FEATHER BLEND

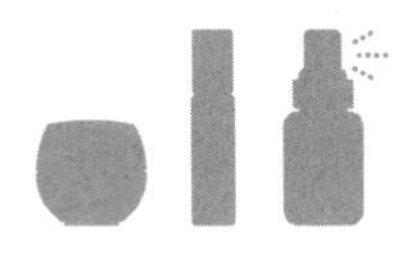

Ingredients

2 Lavender
encourages the peace of mind that comes from finding your true self

1 Arborvitae
This Oil invites individuals to sacrifice their personal will

1 Cedarwood
Supports individuals in realizing that they are not alone

3 Grapefruit
Honor and respect of personal space and emotions

3 Lime
Revitalizing for the the heart and brings light, joy and emotional honesty

1 Cypress
Helps individuals move with the flow of life

2 Geranium
Encourages emotional honesty, love, and enables deeper connection with others

Fractionated Coconut Oil

10ml Rollerball Bottle

3oz Glass Spray Bottle (optional)

Method

Add the Essential Oils to the empty rollerball bottle, fill the rest of the way with Fractionated Coconut Oil, replace the rollerball lid, and roll on your wrists, back of neck, behind the ears, or over your heart to experience the benefits.

You can also diffuse 1-2 drops of each of these Oils, or make a spray by adding 2 drops of each Essential Oil to a 3oz glass spray bottle, fill the rest of the way with water, shake and spray to freshen the room, or on yourself for a scented body mist.

Optional addition:

3 Rose

Provides a feeling of unconditional Divine love, and offers emotional healing for the heart

CHAPTER
ONE

introduction

How long has it been since you've done anything for yourself? I'm willing to bet it's been way too long. I'd love to help you change that.

I know that you may not feel you have *time* to spend on yourself. You may think of self-care as "too expensive" or even an indulgence. You might even feel a little bit (or a lot) of *guilt* about devoting time to just you. I get it...I used to feel the same way.

I've been where you are. I was busy taking care of all the other things---five kids, a husband, a full-time job, and my in-laws, after they were each diagnosed with cancer. I didn't take care of myself, and I ended up with chest pains, headaches, and extra weight to prove it. And that was just the *physical* fallout.

Emotionally, I was drained. My work started feeling like work. I was going through all the motions with a smile on my face, telling those who asked, "I'm fine." But, I wasn't; and I didn't want to allow myself to realize that.

More about me and my journey later, but for now, please know that my experiences drove me to become pretty obsessed with finding easy-to-implement self-care strategies that really worked, and didn't take up too much time, money, or brain power.

I was my own first guinea pig for these fixes. When something worked for me, I passed it along to someone else who needed some help. The things that worked started piling up. I was feeling stronger, and happier…I was sleeping better, I was more active-and feeling less guilty about taking a few minutes for myself.

I have learned that, whether we believe it or not, we all have the power within ourselves to press the re-start button, and start living in a healthier, more positive way. *No matter how far down a path we are, we can always turn around and come back home, finding solace and security in that process.*

Another big thing I learned? Baby steps will get you there. You don't have to make sweeping, drastic changes overnight! Devoting just a few little minutes to yourself can bring about big, positive changes that can affect you beyond what you may think is possible. When you invest in yourself in this way, you allow your inner light to shine, and that light is a beacon for those around you. *Our world needs light.* So, this is not selfish work. It's worthy of your time and resources, because YOU, my friend are worthy, and so deserving of stepping into the happy, healthy life you were meant to live!

During my journey, I have also learned a lot about Essential Oils. Do you know much about them? Have you ever used them? My first exposure to them was walking by vendor tables at wellness events. I used to think, "they smell nice, and if they don't hurt you---great!" I have come to build a deeper relationship with Essential Oils, and now I know them as plant-based medicine. After going from almost no medications in our house to having a whole cabinet full when we were taking care of my father-in-law, I began looking for natural solutions. I don't believe that God would've put us on this planet without giving us everything we need to survive, and thrive. He didn't just stick us here and say, "Well, good luck then…see ya!"

Throughout time, people have used plants and plant materials for physical and emotional health needs and everyday support. Modern science and research have taught us things about how we can use natural, God-given substances to support our bodies and brains with incredible results.

I've seen these results for myself---*in* myself, and in those I care about. As an investigative reporter, I'm trained to ask the right questions and look for facts, and you'd better believe I researched Essential Oils before I decided to open a bottle and give it a try. I was amazed at how quickly a tiny drop was able to help with things so common to so many of us: aches and pains, respiratory issues, digestive issues, immunity support, skin issues, stress, poor quality sleep, and on and on. Now, I put them on me and in me every day. I even cook, and clean with them…and when I started combining Essential Oils with self-care? WOW! It was like finding the missing thing my body and brain were craving! I can't wait to help *you* elevate *your* self-care efforts with them, too.

I want to give you a little primer on Essential Oils, so you feel comfortable using them safely. The first thing we need to do is be smart consumers. Research continues to show that people around the world want natural, environmentally friendly products, and Essential Oils have become wildly popular (again). You no longer have to search for some little holistic store to buy them. Essential Oils are right out there on shelves at grocery stores, discount stores, salons and spas, even gas stations! Companies are jumping in to sell Essential Oils because they want to tap into this big market, and there's a huge variety of quality out there as a result. Not everybody's in it for the same reason. Before you buy Essential Oils, please make sure to take a look at the company behind what you're buying. Is it focused on education, sourcing, testing, and healthcare? That's what you want. Essential Oils are not regulated. That means a bottle labeled "100% Pure" may contain a fraction of a drop that is 100% pure, and the rest is a synthetic filler. I don't want you using a low quality Oil, not getting positive results, and then telling all your friends that "Essential Oils don't work." What I'm going to be helping you with in this book, is based on using the real stuff---pure gifts of this earth.

When we have a pure, therapeutic grade quality of Oil we trust, we can use them in three ways:

AROMATICALLY

JUST BREATHE THEM IN

Whether it's from the bottle, a drop in the palm of your hand, a diffuser, or from a piece of aromatherapy jewelry. Our sense of smell is complex and built to process scents in incredible ways that impact our physical and emotional well-being. When we diffuse Essential Oils, we are also purifying the air in a safe, natural way. Think about the things you buy in spray cans, plug into the wall, or burn to make your home smell good. Those things were created because, very simply, we like nice scents. Also notice that many of them were synthetically made to mimic something in nature. Now, look at the ingredients on those things. Most contain harmful chemicals. You don't have to use those things, you know! There's a safer way. Using a diffuser for your Essential Oils brings *natural* scent into your home, and it breaks the particles down into a very fine mist. When we inhale them, they are easily absorbed into the respiratory system for physical benefits, and the scent also triggers *emotional* reactions in our brains based on our own experiences. If you've ever found yourself feeling happy when you catch a whiff of fresh cut grass because it takes you back to fun times as a child playing outside in the warm summer sun, you know what I'm talking about here.

TOPICALLY

APPLY THEM TO THE SKIN

This is one of the fastest, easiest ways to support your body with Essential Oils. They are wonderful for our skin – our largest organ. Essential Oils enhance the benefits of massage, and can be used in a variety of other ways to soothe, cleanse, and improve your skin. In Chapter 6, I'll show you how you can use Essential Oils to help you start *looking* better as you're feeling better. So many of the skincare and haircare products we use include toxins and fillers. Let's stop rubbing and spraying toxins on ourselves! Various research from years of medical testing shows that toxins we're exposed to everyday in the products we use disrupt the healthy function of our bodies and brain, and pose significant health concerns. Essential Oils are a pure, natural, and safe way to take care of our skin and hair. Essential Oils are potent, and many experts recommend diluting the Oil in a "carrier" which helps to minimize the risk of any skin irritations. This could be Coconut Oil, Avocado Oil, or even a natural serum or moisturizer that you use. It's also important to note that the sun can increase sensitivity. Most citrus Oils, for example, have photosensitive chemical compounds, and it's recommended that we stay out of direct sunlight when we're using them topically. Also, there are some areas that are very sensitive to Essential Oils. We should avoid getting Oils in our eyes, ears, around the genitals, or on damaged/open skin. When you're starting out, go with a very tiny amount (even less than a drop) of Oil, and see how your body is going to react. Children, the elderly, and those with sensitive skin are more likely to develop a sensitivity. You can find links to safety charts at TakeCareTips.com; and please, feel free to ask your doctor about any specific concerns you may have based on your health. Now is probably also a good time to point out that I am not a doctor, and the tips I'm sharing with you in this book shouldn't be a substitute for advice from a medical professional. What I'm passing along here are natural remedies that have worked for me and for people I know, and because of that, I feel comfortable and confident sharing them with you.

INTERNALLY

DRINKING A DROP IN WATER, OR SWALLOWING ESSENTIAL OILS IN A SUPPLEMENT OR CAPSULE

Besides being a great way to add natural flavoring to what we eat and drink, using an Essential Oil internally brings a variety of health benefits, through offering support to your gastrointestinal system, your immune system, your cellular health, and more! As we talked about before, not all Oils are a quality we can trust to use internally, so please make sure to check the bottle carefully. If it is approved for internal use, it will say that! Don't just assume that *anything* labeled Peppermint Oil is OK to put in your tea—using a synthetic blend that way would be like drinking a drop of perfume!

Whether you're using Essential Oils aromatically, topically, or internally, make sure to follow dosage recommendations. And again, if you have any specific questions or concerns, please don't be afraid to bring it up with your healthcare provider. More health professionals are being educated on Essential Oils so they can help their patients who want holistic options. If you need other resources, I have some for you in the back of this book.

With all that said, as of right this minute, you have permission to take care of yourself. Were you waiting for permission? I hope not! But, if you needed to hear it, there it is. *You have permission to take care of yourself!* In fact, tell anyone who dares to give you a hard time that your new friend Jen said that you must spend *at least* ten guilt-free minutes on yourself, every day.

If you're going to be throwing my name around like that, I guess I should tell you little bit about myself. (It might be embarrassing if someone asks for details about your new buddy and you have nothing to say). I am Jennifer Antkowiak. I have a husband, five children of my own, and an older step-daughter (who I also like to think of as my own). I took care of my mother-in-law and father-in-law after they were diagnosed with cancer.

Because I wanted and needed to spend more time taking care of my family, I made the decision to leave the security and regular paycheck of a 23-year career as a TV news anchor and reporter---twice!

Millions around the world find themselves stretched between family and career; and many end up putting family first, even if they don't know exactly how things will work out. Financial questions and concerns add to an already stressful situation.

In leaping, I have learned that, as scary as it may seem, when we step out in faith, we are supported. In choosing to let some things go, other opportunities have presented themselves. I feel like I've been able to "stumble upon" my purpose, and passion. I've created TV shows, magazines, websites, and more to provide information, support, and tools to help people take better care of themselves and those they love, naturally.

Although it sounds like a lot, the beauty and the blessing of it is that I am able to do most of my "work" from home. I feel more in control of my schedule now, and I try very hard to consistently carve out some time for myself. I can tell you from hard-won experience that devoting time to focus on just you is *not* a luxury, it's a *necessity*. If you don't take the time you need to keep yourself strong, there's no way you will ever possibly be strong enough to take care of anyone else. It's really just that simple.

I've also learned to think about caring for myself as a *process*. I don't get it right all the time. I still have nights when I don't get enough sleep, and I still have days when I don't stand firm on giving myself even ten minutes to recharge.

Now, I know your story isn't exactly like mine, but I'll bet we've got a few things in common. I'll bet you're a juggler, too. You have seen how one thing can lead to another, and another. You are different things to different people, and you have probably seen that it's easy to lose yourself in caring for others. I want to help you move up to the front of the line again, because if you put yourself first, you will find that it's so much easier to manage the rest. With *Essential Take Care Tips*, you will see that you don't need to have a lot of time or money to make a difference.

Connecting with people like you fuels me. Often, after my presentations on How to Care for Yourself While You're Taking Care of Others, I have been overwhelmed by those who come up to share their stories:

How incredible that these people were willing to share intensely emotional and personal information, just like that. It speaks to the desperate, very real, very urgent need for help with self-care.

The woman who pushed her mother in a wheelchair up to me – both of them in tears: "Look at her, the mother said to me. "She's young, she's beautiful. All she does is take care of me. She doesn't spend any time on herself. She needs to go out with friends and do things for herself. I feel so guilty that she has to take care of me like this." "Mom, I told you," the daughter said, giving me a teary glance, "I wouldn't want to be anywhere else. I want to take care of you. This is what I want to be doing," Then, to me, "Please help me make her understand."

The out-of-breath, pink-cheeked man in a rumpled shirt who came running in, asking if he had missed my talk. When I told him he had, he asked if I had all the information in a book, or online. "I need help," he told me – and again, some tears. "I live out of town, but I travel back here to take care of my mother. No one else in the family can do it, and to be honest, I don't know if I can do it either."

A woman who nervously and quietly told me, after I gave the presentation in a corporate setting, that she was taking care of her father with Alzheimer's. "I feel so guilty complaining about this," she whispered, "but it is really hard. I'm struggling to stay focused and keep up with everything here at work. I'm not sleeping. I'm gaining weight. I'm a mess. I need help."

Obviously, for each of these people, taking care of a loved one is the most important thing in their lives. However, as they were talking to me, I was worrying about who was taking care of *them*. In my own little world, I have seen so many people walking around with those kinds of intense feelings right beneath the surface, unspoken and unattended-to. All it takes is for someone to open a door, or even just push it a little ajar, and they let everything go and cry for help. Others are walking around in a state of denial, adapting to the new stress levels as their new normal. This is not healthy. It will catch up with you.

It's not likely that a fairy with a magic wand is going to fly in and make everything better in seconds. (I won't rule it out completely, I'm just saying it's not likely). I don't have a magic wand either, but I do have tools that will help.

Make no mistake, we are talking about serious subjects, personal health crisis situations (and we need to address them as such); but my way of thinking is you don't need one more *heavy* thing around you. I'm not going to scare you with tons of research and statistics (OK, well actually I am a little bit here and there, but it's all for the greater good---I want to empower you with knowledge!). Mostly, I'm going to give you practical information that you can use to re-energize your body and your brain, and get back to a feeling of happiness and well-being. Remember what that felt like?

Essential Take Care Tips is organized into chapters that represent key areas of your life you need to focus on to reduce your risks of health problems specifically related to people who care for others more than themselves. You don't have to read this book cover to cover right from the start. I set it up so that if you're having trouble sleeping, for example, you can flip to Chapter 5 and quickly get information that can help. Each chapter will also give you many of my best Ten-Minute Tips and Essential Oil recipes that you can start to use immediately. In a perfect world, we'd all have *unlimited* time, but I know firsthand that in reality, time is a scarce, valuable commodity. So…if you can commit to blocking out just ten little minutes (some of the tips don't even take that long), I'm going to teach you how you can make big, positive changes in your life. Along the way, you'll notice, too, that the areas of your life that you're going to need to focus on are related to lessons that your mother probably tried to get into your head all along. Read through the table of contents again---do the names of any of those chapters sound familiar? Let's look at them again, now that you're an adult. You'll see that some tips work best if you do them every day, others are an every-once-in-a-while thing. You can decide what works best for you. That's the goal –this book is like a big box of tools and I invite you to pick up and try out every single one.

You can do this. I am excited to be here with you. Time for *you* starts right now.

CHAPTER ONE

do your homework

I know you don't have the time to read this book. I'd really like you to do it anyway. I mean, you picked it up for a reason. Why were you drawn to it? There's something you want to change, huh? You're tired and frustrated with feeling like you're working so hard, but not getting very far. You're sick of your never ending To Do list. You want to go to bed relaxed and wake up happy! You don't really feel like you have time to add anything else into your day, but you want things to change.

I want that for you, too. It's time for YOU. It's time to *own* where you are, figure out where you want to go, and learn how to take the action you need to get there. I'm excited for you!

Before we go any further together, I'd like to help you get settled and focused. Close your eyes and take a slow, deep breath in through your nose and then slowly, and gently let it out through your mouth. Keep your shoulders down and relaxed. Give yourself some time and do a few of these. With each breath in, think about taking in all good things…and as you release that breath, think about letting go of anything negative from your day.

Doesn't that feel better? That's a pretty cool way to create a personal happy space, don't you think? It's fast, and free!

That's the feeling I want you to have every time you pick up this book to spend some time with me. Get yourself centered. Block out distractions, and make this your special time to focus on *yourself.* Also, trust that you have everything you need inside yourself to take charge and manage any situation. It's easy to lose sight of that, but it's true. *You have everything you need.* There's such power in believing that!

I am extremely passionate about the messages in this book. My own life-changing caregiving experiences brought me to this path. It is my sincere hope and prayer that something I have learned will help to make your life easier.

MY CAREGIVING STORY

I learned what it was like to be a caregiver at a young age. My mother lived with post-partum depression while I was growing up. Unfortunately, hers didn't get any better with time. The disease was difficult for all of us to understand – my mom, my dad, and my three younger sisters and me. There were good days and bad days. It hurt me horribly to see the bad days. I know in my heart that my mom wanted to be happy and healthy for us, and with us---and I'm afraid that she struggled and suffered even more than I know. It went on for years, with my mom seeing different doctors, and staying in different facilities; with all of us trying to hold down the fort in our own ways.

It was not the life either of my parents had envisioned, and when I was almost done with high school, my parents divorced. Because of my mother's illness, my sisters and I stayed in our house with my dad. My mom had moved in with her mom, about two hours away. She lived there for a couple of years before moving into an apartment back home, closer to my sisters.

By then, I had moved away to college, and throughout those years, besides being a student, I was a long-distance caregiver for my family – helping to relieve some of the pressure from my father, who was working and trying to raise us, and helping my mother and grandmother to manage my mom's care.

Not long after graduation from college, when I was working at a television station in Erie, Pennsylvania, I received a phone call from a police officer in my small home town, telling me that there had been an emergency – something with my mother – and that I needed to call the hospital. I called to check on what happened, and after a long wait, an emergency room nurse came on the phone and told me, "Your mother is no longer with us." "You moved her to a different hospital?" I asked.

"No, I'm sorry, she has passed," the nurse said.

Just like that. No more mom. I found out later that she had a massive heart attack. She was only 50 years old. It was sudden, and shocking, and final. I missed her immediately and deeply; but at the same time I hoped that after living with a troubled mind for all those years, my beautiful mother would find peace.

When my mom died, I was three months away from getting married. We had been looking forward to going out together to shop for the dress she would wear to my wedding. Instead, I was in a daze, going through the motions of picking out clothes, flowers, prayers, and songs, for her funeral.

My mother-in-law-to-be offered me great support during that time. She scooped me up and took me under her wing. She had been orphaned as a child and she knew what it was like to move through life without a mother. She opened her heart to me and surrounded me with her love.

While I know my own mother watches and protects me from above, it was my mother-in-law who was physically here with me to celebrate my early career advancements, and later, for the births of four of our five children. She didn't live to see our last child come into this world.

Like my mother, my mother-in-law (Me-Ma, as I called her) was the ultimate caregiver, and never liked to admit if she was having any problems. Not long after my third son was born I noticed that Me-Ma was short of breath at times, and seemed to be moving at a slower pace. She tried to dismiss it, but one afternoon she called me to say that she hated to bother me (of course) but she was having trouble catching her breath after doing some housework.

"What were you doing?" I asked. "Running up and down the stairs with laundry?"

"Making the bed," she answered.

She was out of breath after just pulling up the covers on the bed. I asked her some questions and her responses sounded to me like they were coming from someone who was close to having a heart attack. I had to convince her to go to the emergency room. Doctors found several blockages. Me-Ma went through quintuple bypass surgery and the long recovery period that followed.

About a year and a half later, shortly after my daughter was born, I noticed that my mother-in-law wasn't eating much, and again seemed out of breath and slow at times. She confided in me that she had been having stomach pains and that she felt very tired. This time, doctors found cancer, a fast-growing kind. No surgery or therapy was recommended. We were told we should get in touch with a Hospice.

When we went back to her house that sunny afternoon, Me-Ma and I sat out on her screened porch (her favorite place) and we talked. "This is pretty bad, isn't it?" she asked. "Let's look at this as an adventure," I said, hopefully. "Nobody knows how much time they have left, but let's make the most of it."

Through the years, Me-Ma had seen how I kept my mother's memory close and her spirit alive, how I shared stories about her with my young children, how I asked her for help when I needed it, and how I felt her with me always. "Do you think it will be like that for you with me?" she asked. "I absolutely do," I said, and she smiled. And after a couple of minutes of silence…"Please take care of Pap," she said.

Pap was my dear father-in-law, who ended up moving in with us. "Of course I will." I told her. "I hate that all of this is on you," she said. "How am I going to repay you for all of this?" I held her hand and told her that my "payment" was the blessing of being with her – and her allowing me into this private time in her life.

"You know how they say that when you get up there, you can pull some strings and help people?" she continued. "Well, if that's true, I want you to know that I will get with your mother and we will do whatever we can to help you…to make your life easier."

Six weeks from that cancer diagnosis, I gave the eulogy at my mother-in-law's funeral mass.

It was my honor to work with a Hospice to take care of her in her home during those six weeks. At the time it was happening, I was just back to work from my fourth maternity leave – back to a full-time, extremely public job as a TV news anchor and reporter. I had three toddlers, an infant, and a husband at home. In those last weeks I would stop at my in-laws' house on the way to work, on the way home, and then again after the kids were tucked into bed. I talked to doctors and looked online to find out everything I could about cancer and how it progresses. I researched medicines. I found myself administering medicines to my mother-in-law, keeping pain charts and lists of reactions to medications and dosages. I helped to organize counseling for family members. I kept a journal with my mother-in-law. I made sure my father-in-law was eating and sleeping. I tried to keep my house, and my in-laws' house, straightened up. I took care of my own family, and continued to breastfeed the baby. I tried to stay connected to what was going on in the world so that I could continue to do what I needed to do at work.

I had a strong sense that I was the one who needed to take care of all those people and things, and I happily did it. I wouldn't have wanted it any other way.

Geez though, what an unhealthy way to live! Looking back on it now, I realize that giving all that care to others meant I wasn't sleeping. I wasn't eating well. I wasn't getting any exercise. I gained weight. My skin was dry (I was probably dehydrated). I had aches and pains I'd never had before. I had headaches. But I kept going with that routine, not even pausing to consider that it was all too much.

Maybe because of my news background, researching what was happening consumed me. I know that knowledge is power, and I wanted to arm myself with as much knowledge as possible so that I could try to keep a step ahead of the situation. I didn't want to be caught off guard. I wanted to be able to remain a source of calm and strength to Me-Ma and the family.

I realize now that it wasn't until after my mother-in-law's funeral that I thought about myself. I was forced to. Not taking care of myself had caught up with me. I had to go to the hospital with chest pains – scared because of my family history of heart disease, including my mother dying of a heart attack at a young age. I was admitted and hooked up to a heart monitor.

Thankfully, my heart checked out OK, but before the doctor released me, he asked me about my lifestyle. He told me my chest pains were related to stress, and to consider them as a big red flag to hit the brakes, and spend some time taking care of myself.

Looking into my little children's eyes when I got home pushed me to listen to the doctor's advice. My children were going to have to grow up without grandmothers, but I would do everything I could to make sure they did not have to grow up without me.

Early on, Hospice nurses and social workers pointed out that by agreeing to be a caregiver for my mother-in-law, I was stepping into a role full of new challenges, and that these new challenges could cause a lot of mental and physical strain. "Don't worry about me, I'll be fine," I said.

How many times have *you* said, "Don't worry about me, I'll be fine?" As caregivers, we don't want to put a spotlight on ourselves. We're not thinking about our own health. We just don't have time. A Hospice doctor I interviewed for this book, Dr. Randy Herbert, who has done quite a bit of research on caregivers, brought out an interesting point about this concept: When you are taking care of someone because they're sick – perhaps terminally ill – you feel sad. And you feel their sadness as well as your own, *because* you care so much. You feel depressed. Those are exactly the normal feelings you should be feeling. A loved one is sick or dying; how else would you feel? Asking you to feel positive and motivated to be healthy is absolutely abnormal in that situation.

So, whether you're taking care of a sick or dying loved one, or you're feeling overwhelmed taking care of healthy people and things in your life, our challenge now is for you to find the strength to be abnormal (and even feel positive – but in an honest, realistic way). That "don't worry about me, I'll be fine" attitude isn't gonna cut it anymore. You have a lot of living to do! Don't allow caring for others to rob you of your wellbeing. Those you are caring for wouldn't want that, and neither do I.

From my own experience I know that it would have been tough if not impossible for someone to say something – anything – that could pull me away from my perceived responsibilities and "force" me to spend some time on myself.

Guess what though? When one caregiving situation is over, there are other people standing there who need your attention. If you wait for "leftover" time to begin taking care of yourself, it will never happen. *You need to make time to take care of yourself* now. You're not alone…you have me to help you, and you know I'm fueled by two strong, wonderful women.

Let me start by sharing some information about this already very *personal*, but also growing *public* health issue.

WHO IS DOING ALL OF THIS CAREGIVING?

Well, the short answer is, women who are not trained to be doing it. Stories like mine are being played out right now by at least 63 million people in America. Most of them are women. Most are in their mid to late 40s, although we are seeing a lot of growth in younger and elderly caregiver groups. More and more men are also stepping into caregiver roles. Most caregivers have families and jobs. The majority have a high school degree, and no formal health care training. Most have health problems of their own. Many have either lost or run the risk of losing their health insurance because their caregiving schedule forces them to either quit or reduce their hours of work outside the home. Most caregivers aren't getting the support they would like to be confident in caring for their loved ones. As the health care system becomes more and more strained, daily care is falling more and more on the shoulders of family caregivers. In fact, it's estimated that family caregivers are providing ongoing care to nearly 80% of the chronically ill in America!

There's huge economic impact to this situation as well.

Most family caregivers provide their services free of charge, but studies show that if all those caregivers were paid for their services – cooking, cleaning, administering medications, helping with basic hygiene, working out financial difficulties, managing health insurance, providing transportation, offering mental and physical help, etc. – they'd be earning nearly 300 billion dollars a year! These numbers are growing by the minute; and they will continue to go up as our population continues to age (the numbers go up immediately if you agree with me that taking care of healthy people makes you a caregiver too).

Now, I'd guess that you're not looking to put a monetary value on your service, but still, it's an important fact. Those statistics speak loud and clear about the volume of volunteer caregiving. What you do is a big deal, remember that. Just be aware that while you're putting out all that time and energy looking after others, you could be taking a big chance with your own health.

"I'LL BE FINE."

When you don't take care of your own health needs, you put yourself at a higher risk – in some cases more than double the risk – for a variety of serious mental and physical diseases, as well as for dying at a younger age! Many times the early signs and symptoms are there but the caregiver ignores them, making the problem more difficult to treat later on.

Medical research shows that those of us who are caregivers are almost twice as likely to develop heart disease and/or have a heart attack. We are almost twice as likely to develop diabetes, depression, and even cancer. We are more likely to be overweight or obese. We are also at risk for less serious diseases including chronic headaches, muscular pain, arthritis, colds and flu, and acid reflux.

These increased risks come directly as the result of the caregiving lifestyle. We aren't sleeping or eating well. Our stress levels are through the roof. Getting out to exercise just doesn't happen. Those negative patterns lead to problems with the immune system, and an increase in amount and severity of infections.

The stress that comes with caregiving can take ten years off your life! Prolonged stress causes a variety of other issues in the body as well. Stress makes the heart and all the organs work harder. Caregivers are at a greater risk for developing high blood pressure.

This is scary stuff. I'm not telling you this to create more stress in your life. I'm telling you this because I want you to be aware of the facts regarding what you face if you continue with a routine that doesn't include self-care. The good news is, you have the power to turn things around and reduce your health risks. I'm committed to helping you with that.

BASIC CARE FOR CAREGIVERS

Let's go over some basic healthcare housekeeping tips. First, take a look at recommendations from traditional, mainstream medical guidelines:

- ○ Make sure your immunizations are up-to-date.
- ○ Get a pneumonia vaccine.
- ○ Get a yearly physical.

- ◯ Tell your doctor that you are a caregiver – this is so important. Saying this buzzword at the outset should send a strong message to your doctor, telling him or her to look at you in a different way. Saying that you're a caregiver will alert your doctor that you are dealing with higher than normal levels of stress, and that you need some extra care and attention. If you don't sense this is happening---get a new doctor!
- ◯ Tell your doctor if you're feeling depressed or nervous. Even if you wouldn't label yourself clinically depressed (a lot of us are and don't even know it), mention any sleeping or eating problems, or feelings of sadness, helplessness, or hopelessness that don't go away. New therapies and medicines have made depression easier to treat. Don't be afraid of a diagnosis. Get help.
- ◯ Take a daily multi-vitamin (ask your doctor or pharmacist if you have any questions about which formula would be best for you).
- ◯ Get a tetanus booster every ten years.
- ◯ Get the recommended cancer screenings based on your age and family history.
- ◯ Get your flu shot once a year (if you have questions or concerns ask your doctor).

Now let's take a look at how a holistic doctor thinks of basic annual care. Loyola Medicine family physician Dr. Kit Lee offers these Holistic Lifestyle Guidelines to boost health and potentially reduce the need for medications (shared with permission from Loyola University Medical Center):

Pay Attention to Sleep Hygiene: Sleep in a cool, dark room. Aim for 7-8 hours a night. Do some gentle stretches to relax the body and help with sleep. Avoid vigorous exercise, alcohol and caffeine before bedtime. Lavender Essential Oil can be calming before sleep. A melatonin supplement can be used occasionally to reset the sleep-and-wake cycle.

Mindful Eating: Take your time when eating to chew slowly, savor the smell, taste and texture, and don't overeat.

Eat a Plant-based Diet: Limit animal-based foods and carbs. Eat mostly vegetables, fruits, whole grains, legumes, seeds and nuts. Fruits and vegetables provide different nutrients and phytochemicals (disease-fighting compounds found in plants).

Take a time out: Spend at least 20 minutes a day in a quiet space that allows you to express your inner voice.

Nature's cure: Spending time outside improves mood, lowers stress hormones, reduces blood pressure., and may boost immunity - plants emit chemicals called phytocides that protect it. When you breathe in phytocides, it increases the level of the immune system's natural killer cells. Getting sunlight helps regulate circadian rhythm (your body's 24-hour internal clock).

Move it!: Adults should do 2 1/2 to 5 hours per week of moderate-intensity aerobic activity or 75 to 150 minutes of vigorous-intensity activity as well as doing muscle-strengthening activities at least twice a week. Check with your physician before beginning a new exercise routine.

Yoga: Physical benefits include increased flexibility, muscle strength and tone, protection against injury, improved balance, better sleep, improved mood and stress relief.

Help Others: Acts of kindness provide multiple health benefits, including lowering blood pressure, boosting self-esteem and relieving stress.

Magic Words: Nurture your personal relationships by saying "thank you", "I love you" and "I'm sorry" often.

Glass Half Full: Having a positive attitude can help manage stress, which can lead to many health benefits, including better heart health, lower rates of depression and improved coping skills.

In the Introduction, I promised you my very best guilt-free ten minute tips to inspire you, and to allow you to start feeling results right away – no matter what's going on in your life.

Let's start with creating your map, and some tips for setting and holding on to your personal goals. This is a fun part where you get to decide what you want more of in your life! Even if you already know about goal-setting, chances are you're not taking all the proven action needed to get what you want. Don't beat yourself up about that---that's the case for most of us. Let's spend a little time getting your plan in place, then we'll talk about putting yourself in a new, energized state of mind as you set the intent and begin a journey to better self-care.

ESSENTIAL TAKE CARE TIP

#1 Set a Goal

Where are you now? Where do you want to go? These are basic questions that should be easy to answer…but they're not! Often, we are so wrapped up in taking care of everyone else that we completely lose sight of what we want for ourselves. So, we really might not know "where we want to go". On top of that, you're probably realizing that as much as you want things to be different, it's going to require some change, and change can be uncomfortable for some; and even intimidating! BUT---changing habits is probably exactly what you need to do to start feeling better, and that's what we'll do here in little, manageable chunks. That will be enough to get you there…I promise! So, don't think about trying to "snap out" of your present situation; instead, think about chipping away at feeling better one day – maybe even one minute – at a time. You will see and feel results, others will too, and that will help you stay on track.

Our bodies and brains are amazing machines! When you start feeding them in a healthy way, with positive thoughts and natural remedies, they will respond. There may be *a lot* of things you want to change---and that's OK! ---, but we've got to start somewhere, and studies show our brains work best when we focus on one thing at a time. Take ten minutes to think about a *first* goal you'd like to achieve to take better care of yourself. It could be about health, fitness, a creative project, relationships, spiritual development, time for reading, travel… anything. Just pick one thing…what's your biggest need right now?

Essential Oils will support you on this part of the journey by helping you focus, and open your heart and mind so that you can reflect on what you really want.

I love an aromatic use of Essential Oils for this work, because it's convenient, easy, and the results are often immediate. We know that simply breathing in an Essential Oil from the bottle, adding a drop to the palm of your hand, rubbing your palms together, cupping them over your nose and mouth and taking relaxed breaths; or placing a few drops of Oils in a diffuser and breathing it in from the air can uplift our mood, and help us to manage our emotions. Our sense of smell is powerful. Just breathing in an Essential Oil triggers a reaction with chemical sensors in the brain which creates a response. We're wired for this! Let's tap into that to get clear on our plan.

Are you struggling a bit to set a goal for yourself? Get your Lemon Oil, which is known as a cleansing Oil, and an Oil that helps with focus. It supports your mind with the energy it needs to find clarity. It's also said to help release feelings of hopelessness, and bring back feelings of belief in yourself. As you breathe in your Lemon Oil, ask yourself questions like:

What do I want to experience more of right now?

If I was experiencing that thing, how would it make a difference in my life?

How serious am I about committing to make the changes needed to bring this into my life?

Let yourself go with the answers to those questions. Allow yourself to really think about how things around you will change when *you* change. Get as detailed as possible. How will you wake up? What will you do in the morning? What will your room smell like…feel like? What clothes will you wear? What will you think when you look in the mirror? What will your relationships feel like? What kinds of things will you do during your day?

Write your thoughts in a journal. That will help to keep those visions alive, and those visions will be the things that keep you connected to your goal, even on the rough days.

Other Oils to Help with Focus & Clarity:

- Basil
- Bergamot
- Cedarwood
- Lavender
- Lemongrass
- Peppermint
- Rosemary
- Sandalwood
- Vetiver

Here's a blend that will help you stay focused. Make it as needed to support you in keeping away distractions as you work to find clarity about what will bring you joy:

FOCUS BLEND

Ingredients		Method
2	Lavender Essential Oil	Following the manufacturer's instructions that came with your diffuser, fill your diffuser with water, then add the drops of Oils. Turn on the mist to create a space that supports calm focus.
2	Lemon Essential Oil	
1	Sandalwood Essential Oil	

ESSENTIAL TAKE CARE TIP

#2 Take Yourself Off Hold

Maybe you've set goals before, but you let them slip away by not taking action. Many people don't take action because they don't know where to start, and allow themselves to become kind of paralyzed. Let's fix that. Take yourself off hold by outlining a list of specific steps you can take to get closer to achieving your goals.

Take ten minutes on a regular basis to keep a record of how you're doing. Ideally, see if you can do this at the end of every day, but do it at least once a week.

Lavender Essential Oil will support you as you are honest about what you truly want for yourself. Apply a drop on your heart to calm any guilt, tension or fear as you step into this space of making your own self a priority. Keep a section in your journal for this. Visit the Free Resources area at www.TakeCareTips.com to download your GOALS planner worksheet, or you can lay it out in your journal like this: the first part will be your reminder to keep your Big Picture Goals front and center as you move through each day. Then, the Progress Check will get you into action.

BIG PICTURE GOALS

PROGRESS CHECK

My health goal:	My family/home goal:	My business/financial goal:
....	....	....
....	....	....
....	....	....
....	....	....
....	....	....
....	....	....
....	....	....
I will achieve this goal by this date:	I will achieve this goal by this date:	I will achieve this goal by this date:
....	....	....

One thing I can do today to move closer to:

My health goal:	My family/home goal:	My business/financial goal:
....	....	....

....

....

....

Celebrate your accomplishments!

- Be grateful for the things that are going right today.
- Remind yourself that you are as exactly as strong as you need to be to achieve your goals.

ESSENTIAL TAKE CARE TIP

#3 Better Breathing

We've become a society of shallow-breathers! When I'm telling you that we're taking care of others to the point that we aren't taking care of ourselves, I mean on base levels---like we're not even giving ourselves enough oxygen! Simply taking the time to focus on getting a few good, deep breaths can change your body and your brain, instantly! The increased oxygen will give your brain a boost. It also helps to relax your muscles and your mind. That's job #1! Everything else follows.

This little breathing exercise is a great way to start your day, but any time is good.

1. Find a few minutes to sit quietly.

2. Place your feet flat on the floor.

3. Rest your hands comfortably in your lap. Sit up straight. Relax your shoulders.

4. Close your eyes. Let everything else go and think about only your breathing.

5. Breathe in slowly and deeply through your nose.

My friend, Health Psychologist Nancy Mramor suggests making a mental note of the number of seconds you normally take for a breath. Hold that air in for a little bit, and then let it all flow out through your mouth. Be aware of how long that takes. Allow yourself to increase those numbers even by a second or two. Over time, you will increase your lung capacity. Taking a few minutes for deep breathing exercises like this will help you to relieve stress and re-energize for the rest of the day.

Our cells need oxygen to survive and thrive, and Lemon, Lavender, and Peppermint Essential Oils work together to provide respiratory support. Add 10 drops of each to a 10ml glass rollerball bottle and top it off with Fractionated Coconut Oil. Rub the blend on your sinuses, chest, or back. You can also diffuse 3-5 drops of a pre-made Respiratory Blend of Oils including Laurel Leaf, Peppermint, Eucalyptus, Tea Tree, Lemon, Ravensara, and Cardamom; or massage a drop of one of those Oils, or that blend into the bottom of each foot to support your respiratory system. Because this blend contains a citrus, it is advised, due to photosensitivity, not to expose the area of the skin that citrus Oil has been applied to, for at least 12 hours after application.

IF YOU WANT MORE:

Allow yourself to practice this kind of breathing as much as possible, specially when you feel a lot of anxiety or stress brewing. Keep your respiratory support Oils handy for those times, too.

ESSENTIAL TAKE CARE TIP

#4 Accentuate The Positive

Sometimes we can get stuck in our troubles, wallowing around with other people who are happy to wallow with us. How helpful is that?! Take ten minutes right now to go through your address book and friends list and seek out positive people. Those are the ones you want to hang out with! Call one of them and share that you are realizing you haven't been doing enough to take care of yourself and you are working to change that. Tell them you'd love to get together with them because you want to be around positive people! Chances are good that some friends have been wanting to reach out to you but didn't know how to start. Show them an open door.

Tea Tree Oil is an Oil I have grown to know and love for help with placing yourself in a protective bubble, and keeping negative energy away. I must admit I was not fond of the scent at first, and was interested to hear an aromatherаperist say that often times, the Oils that "don't agree with us" are the ones we need the most! I learned that Tea Tree is known for being an Oil that supports creating boundaries, and helps us to let go. Apply a drop around your belly button to feel empowered to make the choices you need to make to cut the sand bags and soar!

ESSENTIAL TAKE CARE TIP

#5 Do Something You used to Love to Do

(SIMPLE PLEASURES)

Instead of collapsing on the couch in front of the TV for a break, take ten minutes to do something more active that feeds your inner child or your romantic self: Hold hands with someone you care about and go for a walk – or go play in the backyard with the kids or the dog. It doesn't have to be a whole afternoon; even a few minutes of doing something that brought you happiness in the past has a good chance of putting you back in touch with that sense of joy again. You will feel better fast, and that will make it easier for you to do things for yourself more often.

One of the saddest things I encounter when talking with people who haven't been taking care of themselves in a while is that they actually forget what brings them joy! Wild Orange Essential Oil is bright, cleansing, and encourages you to lighten up, laugh, and recognize all the good things you have around you. You can diffuse a few drops of Wild Orange, or add a drop to aromatherapy jewelry to keep those good feelings with you as you move through your day. A spicy, warm pre-made blend of Oils known as the Inspiring Blend includes Cinnamon Bark, Cardamom, Ginger, Clove, Sandalwood, Jasmine, and Vanilla Bean. It helps you light a fire within yourself again! Diffuse it, or apply to pulse points, like your wrists, inside of elbows, and the back of your neck.

IF YOU WANT MORE:

Please do make it an afternoon! Allow yourself even more guilt-free time to go to a movie, a ballgame, or take a craft class. That may require some planning ahead, but do it for yourself. It will work wonders, and the positive effects will stay with you for a while!

ESSENTIAL TAKE CARE TIP

#6 Keep Your Eye On The Prize

As you're deciding to make your own health and wellness a priority, you've got to ask yourself an important question. Do you feel you're worth it? I believe with my whole heart that you are...but in the end, it doesn't matter what I think. This is about you, and I know that for you to be able to move to a place of more control, energy, and joy, you need to feel that you deserve to live that way!

My amazing friend Desiree Mangandog uses Chinese Medicine, energy work, and Essential Oils to help people release emotional baggage and transition to exciting and powerful new feelings of self-worth. Her popular books, I am Fabulous, and I am Worthy guide people through a variety of holistic protocols for healing. As a mom, Desiree can understand how finding time for self-care can feel like a struggle.

"Let's face it, the day can pass you by with work, appointments, traffic, cooking, cleaning, and getting the kids to bed," she told me. But, then she asks, "What are we fighting against that something as basic as nourishing ourselves is hard to accomplish?"

She says she knows the answer: "It's the feelings of shame that keep us busy... our inner critic has a way of reminding us of all the ways we have failed and fallen short. Shame is what needs to shift out of our spirit, so we can move from that feeling of worthless to worthy."

Desire goes on to say, "you are worthy and deserving of physical, emotional, and spiritual health. You matter. The world needs to see your divine worth, to be uplifted and evolve into your highest self. Then you can create and solve problems for our world from a full cup. When you feel it in your bones that you matter, then self-care is as important as breathing. Self-care becomes a "must" and not a "should".

Desiree created this self-care Essential Oil protocol just for Essential Take Care Tips! You can do this I Am Worth It protocol to release shame out of your spirit and begin accepting the magnificent soul that is you.

I am Worth It Protocol

Siberian Fir with Copaiba:
One drop each on the bottom of each foot.
One drop each on the back of your neck.

Lemongrass:
One drop on your heart.

Magnolia:
Roll on inside of elbow creases, wrist creases, and inhale from your hands for one minute.

CHAPTER
TWO

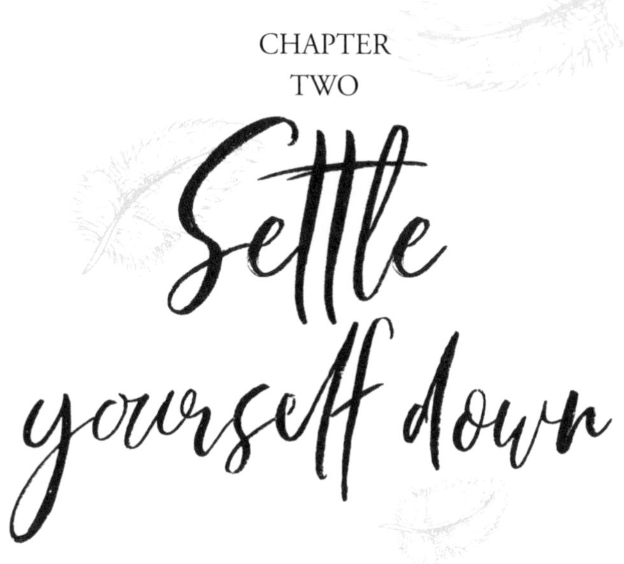

The kids, your spouse, your boss, your friends...you give a lot of yourself to others. You only have so much to give! Many of us care for others to the point that we end up putting our own health and well-being on the back burner. Little by little, we lose pieces of ourselves which can lead to us walking around in an almost constant state of low level stress. Unfortunately, that's common in our world today. It's dangerous, too. And, as more and more people find themselves in the role of family caregiver, the medical community is recognizing the unhealthy fall-out. **Have you been:**

Exhausted, but can't seem to be able to get more than a few hours of sleep a night?

Frustrated with how hard you work, but you can't seem to get ahead?

Gaining weight, or just not feeling good about your body?

Feeling stress or worry most days?

That's no way to live!

- Imagine waking up feeling rested and ready to go, because you got such a good night's sleep...
- You have the time you need to get ready and you feel good about how you look...
- You eat a healthy breakfast, which only adds to your positive energy...
- During the day, you feel happy, confident, and sharp...
- You are able to make decisions...
- You are able to handle any surprises that pop up with family, friends, or work throughout the day...
- You make it a point to fit exercise into your day, and you actually look forward to the feeling it brings! It doesn't feel like you have to drag yourself to get it done, because you like what you're doing, and you love the results you're feeling and seeing in your body...
- You spend time with your family and friends, and you're really in the moment with them, instead of mentally going over your To Do list, and worrying about how much time you're "losing" while you're having a little fun...

You CAN have this kind of a life---you just need to make it a priority. The tools in this book will support you.

Being alive and feeling stress go hand in hand. It's pretty much impossible to live a completely stress-free life, and even if it were possible, you probably wouldn't want to. Stress is a gift, actually. It can be a positive influence in our lives by adding urgency, energy, and excitement. But when we let those feelings get out of control, the problems start emotionally and physically. Our bodies just aren't equipped to handle long term stress. We need to find ways to rest and relax to give ourselves a break. Chronic stress causes harm to every system in the body.

Instead of trying to "eliminate" stress from your life, think about how to manage it. Although we don't have the ability to control everything that happens to us, we do have the power to control our reactions.

I try to teach my kids about this way of thinking. Sports seems to give me the opportunity to do it. You're playing basketball and the referee makes a bad call. What are you going to do about it? Are you going to stomp and pout, and waste valuable game time with that behavior? Or, are you going to quickly accept (agree with it or not) that that's the call that was made, and move into working with the time you have left to get the positive outcome you want?

How can you begin to manage stress in that powerful way? You have everything you need inside.

WHAT IS STRESS EXACTLY?

Although we each could probably give slightly different definitions about what "triggers" us, the word stress generally represents the emotional and physical strain that happens in our bodies and our brains when we respond to pressure we feel around us.

Emotionally, we can respond to pressure by feeling tense, irritable, fatigued, or unfocused. Or sleepless. (That's a big deal! We'll talk about insomnia in Chapter 5.)

Physically, stress can cause you to have a dry mouth, a fast, hard heartbeat, breathing problems, a sick stomach, sweaty palms, and tight, painful, sometimes jittery muscles.

In the Introduction, I told you that soon after my mother-in-law died I had to go to a hospital emergency room with chest pains. My heart felt like it was going to pound out of my chest. I was nauseated. My hands were kind of clammy. My arms and legs were shivering. I was scared to death, sure that I was having a heart attack. Plus, remember, my mother died of a heart attack when she was only 50, so I had the family heart history to worry about, too.

At the ER they started out treating me like a heart patient, but test after test came back negative (thank God), and in the end it was determined that my heart is healthy, and all of my symptoms were stress-related. The cardiologist told me, in no uncertain terms, to get a plan to manage the stress in my life. Notice he didn't tell me to eliminate it...he said "manage". We all need to embrace and manage stress as part of our changing lives. That was the start of my own education about stress. Each of us has our own way of responding to it, so we need to study ourselves a bit to figure how to change things:

- Our personality plays a part: People who constantly push themselves, or are especially assertive and/or aggressive may be more likely to develop stress-related problems.
- Our career plays a part: Demanding jobs like caregiving, medical personnel and public safety personnel are, of course, more likely than others to experience stressful situations.
- Our family history plays a part: If mental illness has shown up in your family, you could be more prone to stress-related problems.

By observing how you react and respond to particular stressors in your life, you can create your own personal early-warning system. You'll start to recognize the mental and physical red flags that let you know it's time to put on the brakes and do what you can to relieve the stress you're feeling – before it overwhelms you and turns into a major problem. The earlier you catch it, the easier it is to fix.

WHAT DOES STRESS DO TO ME?

Stress is one of those built-in human responses that takes us back and connects us with our most basic and primitive animal instincts. I'm talking about the Fight or Flight responses in our body. If you were out in the woods and a wolf approached you, baring its teeth, would you stay and fight it off, or would you run away? When we feel stress, what we feel is our body ramping up to do one or the other, with everything we've got. Our amazing bodies were created to produce a super boost of energy in the face of danger, and to act at top levels. No batteries required.

When a stressful situation like that hits us head on, the brain sounds an alarm and sends out stress hormones like adrenaline, norepinephrine and cortisol. These hormones increase blood flow to the brain and muscles by as much as 400 percent! The heart beats faster. Breathing is faster (which brings more oxygen to the muscles and the brain). The muscles tense. Digestion shuts down (so as not to take any needed energy away from the rest of the body).

In the modern world, there are some times that this fight or flight response can be very helpful. It's what's behind the stories you see on the news (I covered a few myself, actually) where a person was able to move heavy beams to escape a burning building, for example. In instances like this, our stress hormones are working at full power. The stress response is a wonderful thing during these moments... it provides the energy we need to get the job done, and bring our stress levels back down to normal. However, it's not every day – or even every lifetime – that we meet up with a wolf in the woods, or are trapped in a burning building. Even though the stressful situations we deal with on a daily or weekly basis may not be as dramatic, they are intense enough to call out those powerful stress hormones. If we don't have a wolf to fight, or a heavy beam to move, what are we going to do with all of that extra energy? If we don't find a way to manage it, or get rid of it, it'll swirl around inside us and do physical harm. Also, the more we activate those stress hormones, the harder it is for our brains to turn them off. So chronic, low-grade stress can have powerful negative emotional effects, too.

There's no doubt that stress is related to illness. In fact, recent studies show that 60 to 90 percent of illness is brought on by stress!

Some common stress-induced medical problems include:

- Migraines
- Ulcers
- Heartburn and Acid Reflux
- High blood pressure
- Heart disease
- Diabetes
- Asthma
- PMS
- Obesity
- Infertility
- Irritable Bowel Syndrome

Stress is also to blame for causing new, big health problems for people, because too many turn to cigarettes, drugs, alcohol or food for short-term fixes for relief. But that kind of "stress relief" can make the situation much worse, because it doesn't touch the root cause, and can actually leave a person more stressed out than they were to begin with.

WHAT CAUSES STRESS?

Change of any kind can be a major cause of stress – the negative change related to losing a job, for example, but also the positive change that comes with a wedding.

In 1967, two psychiatrists, Thomas Holmes and Richard Rahe, came together to work on a project that would help others be able to figure out if the stressful events they were experiencing could cause health problems.

They interviewed 5,000 people who were being treated for some kind of medical issue. The doctors asked the patients to go through a list of different life events and check the ones that applied to them. Each life event was assigned a score (kind of a stress meter) and they developed a point system that would help to evaluate and estimate a person's health risks based on stress levels.

The Holmes and Rahe Stress Scale is still supported and used today. It's interesting that many, many caregiving-related issues show up on this scale. Want to get a handle on how your stress may impact your health? Check off the things that you've experienced within the past year. Then add up the points for each.

Death of a spouse	100	Marriage	50
Divorce	73	Dismissal from work	47
Marital separation	65	Marital reconciliation	45
Imprisonment	63	Retirement	45
Death of a close family member	63	Change in health of family member	44
Personal injury or illness	53	Pregnancy	40

Sexual difficulties	39
Gain a new family member	39
Business readjustment	39
Change in financial state	38
Change in frequency of arguments	35
Major home mortgage	32
Foreclosure of mortgage or loan	30
Change in responsibilities at work	29
Child leaving home	29
Trouble with in-laws	29
Outstanding personal achievement	28
Spouse starts or stops work	26
Begin or end school	26
Change in living conditions	25
Revision of personal habits	24
Trouble with boss	23
Change in working hours or conditions	20
Change in residence	20
Change in schools	20
Change in recreation	19
Change in church activities	19
Change in social activities	18
Minor mortgage or loan	17
Change in sleeping habits	16

Source: Thomas Holmes and Richard Rahe. Homes-Rahe Social Readjustment Rating Scale, Journal of Psychosomatic Research. Vol II, 1967.

TOTAL: ....

- **Score of 300+: At risk of illness.**
- **Score of 150-299+: Risk of illness is moderate.**
- **Score 150-: Slight risk of illness.**

It's important to point out here that not all stress is caused by things on the outside.

We can be pretty good at generating stress on our own. Things like worry, self-criticism, low self-esteem, and pessimism are all common internal causes of stress. Also, note how many good things are on the list of stressors: marriage, vacation and retirement, for example. It's easy to forget this, and then we wonder why we're so wiped out from something that was supposed to make us feel better.

HOW CAN I MANAGE MY STRESS?

It all comes down to, first, training yourself to get better at identifying what causes you to feel stress. Then, work to let go of as many of those things as possible, and create a healthy plan for how to react to the stress that still does come your way. Remember, the goal is not to eliminate stress, but to manage it.

Focusing on learning how to relax so that stress doesn't cause us to lose joy and hope is so critical for our overall wellness! Think of it as an ongoing quest for balance. No one technique will work for everyone. No one technique will work for you every time. You'll need to experiment to find what makes you feel calm and centered.

This is important work. If you are feeling symptoms of stress, this is your opportunity to put on the brakes and make managing it a priority. By making time for yourself to practice stress relief, you are helping yourself to stay strong when dealing with life's challenges.

And all it costs me is ten minutes? you ask. That's enough to get you started! What a bargain.

Give your stress wings and let it fly away

– Terri Guillemets

INTIMACY AND STRESS

When we are under a lot of stress, our relationships suffer. At the root of this is our relationship with ourselves. When we're not loving ourselves, we really can't be involved in healthy relationships with others, but this is another area we need to work on. Human beings need each other. Our bodies and brains crave intimacy, and one of the many reasons we feel those desires is because when we are physically close with someone we care about, we get something else we need---our brains are wired to release powerful feel-good, stress relieving hormones!

Numerous psychological studies have shown a variety of links between sex and stress management. The focused touching and deeper breathing that comes with physical intimacy calms the mind, and has actually been shown to support healthy blood pressure and heart rate, as well.

The challenge with getting all of these benefits, is that honestly, when you're rundown, it can be pretty tough to feel sexy. The stressful situations in our lives pull us in the opposite direction. We feel physically and emotionally drained. In that state, it can seem easier to just let intimacy go, and one night can lead to a week, and then to a month, and before you know it, you don't remember the last time you were close with someone.

I encourage you not to let your stress ruin your sex life! Everything I'm teaching you in this book is to get you back on track with self-care…eating better, reducing your stress, getting quality sleep, exercising, spending time on your appearance…all of that is going to make you stronger and feel better about yourself, which in turn will help to increase libido. Beyond that, have fun reconnecting with your partner. Talk about what's been bothering you, and that you want to find a way to be close again. If you've been having trouble sexually, just learning that a change in feelings about, or desire for intimacy can be a normal symptom of stress can help a great deal. Breaking through the barrier and allowing yourself to fill that physical need again will help you feel better. To re-establish that connection, some people need to take things slowly---make time for dates where you can laugh together, and build back up to the level of intimacy you want. For others, things move faster after just opening up the discussion. Do what feels right for both of you.

We can reach for Essential Oils to support the desire for physical intimacy. In fact, that's one of the ways ancient Egyptians used them. The floral scents of Rose, Jasmine, Ylang Ylang, and Neroli Essential Oils are known to enhance libido. You can add two drops of each to a diffuser for an aromatherapy experience, or add them to a 10ml roller ball bottle and top it off with Fractionated Coconut Oil to use with massage. If the floral scent is too heavy for you or your partner, you can soften it by adding a drop or two of any citrus Oil, and/or Cedarwood or Sandalwood.

If all else fails, consult a physician. Recent advances in therapies have produced much success in treating sexual dysfunction.

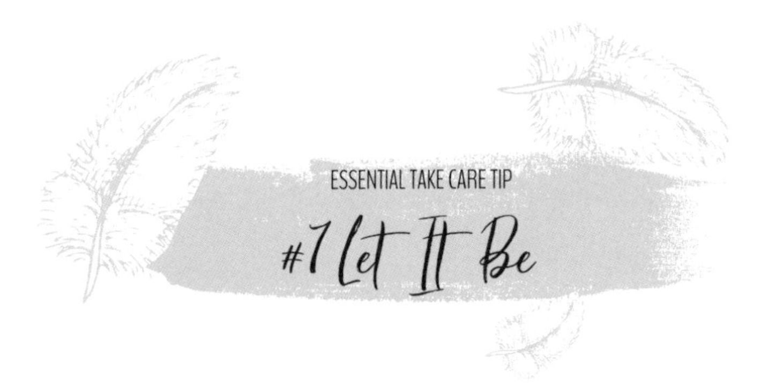

Many wonderful poets have written about the idea that you simply can't change some things, so you need to accept them as they are. This is a big concept, and process. It's not like there's a switch you can flip to all of a sudden just be OK with hard to handle situations. What we want to work for here, is getting to a place where we are choosing to allow what we can't change to just be there without feeling debilitating anger, or sadness around it. It's about giving yourself permission to feel whatever you feel about a stressful situation, and let that be

OK. Honestly, being able to bring yourself to a place of such serene acceptance is probably not going to happen in ten minutes, but I included this concept here because there are some things that you definitely can do in just a few minutes that will help you to chip away at the hurt and anger you may feel when faced with an unchangeable situation. In ten minutes or less you can sit yourself down and:

- Make a list of three things you CAN control about how you react to the situation. (The referee made a bad call. What are you going to do?)
- Try to think of one positive opportunity that could come out of the situation. Maybe a chance for some personal growth?
- Talk about it. Call someone who cares about you, and let them know how you're feeling. It won't change the situation, but hearing some understanding words can help you manage your feelings.

There are several citrus, tree, and herb Essential Oils that support feelings of acceptance: Arborvitae, Bergamot, Juniper Berry, Myrrh, and Thyme all help with releasing the burden of a situation, finding peace with it, and moving on. And, here's a diffuser blend that will help, too:

'I'm ok with this' Blend

Ingredients		Method
3	Bergamot	Following the manufacturer's instructions that came with your diffuser, fill your diffuser with water, then add the drops of Oils. Turn on the mist to create a space that supports acceptance.
2	Patchouli	
1	Eucalyptus	

ESSENTIAL TAKE CARE TIP

#8 Activate Your Relaxation Response

The relaxation response is the exact opposite of the fight or flight response. I'm talking about an active mental process that you can learn, practice and train yourself to do anytime, anywhere. With it, you can trigger reactions in your brain and body that will help bring you back into balance. Your breathing will become slower and deeper. Your heart rate will become slower. Your muscles will loosen up a bit. You're left with a relaxed body and focused brain.

There are several things you can do to achieve the relaxation response, including deep breathing (see Essential Take Care Tip #3 in Chapter 1), and meditation. There have been a lot of studies on the benefits of meditation. There's a long list of things meditation has been found to help with, including: reducing stress, improving concentration, increasing self-awareness and happiness, and slowing aging! Now, if you think that meditation is just too far out there for you, I think you should think again. Many people are finding the value of taking a mental vacation with meditation. It's an ages-old way of quieting the noise of our busy minds, and the outside world, in order to experience the peace inside – a stress-less, interior calm. Many people like to start and/or end their day with meditation, but it works anytime…anywhere!

Find a quiet place – a garden, your bedroom or maybe your church. Get into a comfortable seated position. Pick something to focus on (either a single word or short phrase that you can say, or a special object that you can look at).

Then breathe. Find your focal point, and urge your mind to experience only the moment you're in. No worries about the past or the future. Connect with the stillness of the time and space around you in that particular minute. Let yourself be aware of your breathing and how it makes you feel.

When you first try this, it will take a lot of mental energy to keep your thoughts from wandering. But, the more you practice, the stronger your brain will become, and you will be able to realize deep, long-lasting calming benefits from your meditation time.

Frankincense Essential Oil is wonderful to use during meditation. You can diffuse it, or just apply a drop to your forehead, back of neck, or wrists. Frankincense is said to support a spiritual connection, as well as feelings of being safe and protected.

ESSENTIAL TAKE CARE TIP

#9 Self-Massage

Rubbing your muscles increases blood flow to them and helps to relieve muscle tension. It's a feel good way to boost your energy, too. Although a professional massage is most therapeutic, you can enjoy some of the same relaxing benefits with simple techniques you can do at home. Visit www.TakeCareTips.com to learn about massage techniques.

For sore shoulders: Stretch one arm across the front of your body, reach your opposite hand up and firmly rub the muscle above your shoulder blade. Switch sides and repeat. Finish with giving yourself a hug. Cross your arms in front and grab opposite shoulders. Squeeze and release a few times and feel the tension melt away. Massage a drop or two of Lavender Essential Oil into your shoulders to deepen the soothing benefit.

- Stress can make it hard for us to digest our food. To help with digestion: After a meal, place your palm on your belly and slowly rub in a clockwise motion. That's the direction that food travels through your intestine. Help it along with this simple circular rub. Ginger or Peppermint Essential Oil, and/or a pre-made Digestive Blend of Essential Oils can go to work quickly to support a healthy digestive system. Rub a drop on your belly to gently ease digestive discomfort.

- For the feet: Put some golf balls in a plastic shoe box. Treat your feet by slipping off your shoes and placing them one at a time into the box, and rubbing them over the golf balls. This is a tip to share with the person you're caring for, as well. Massaging a drop of Black Pepper Essential Oil into the bottoms of your feet will warm and soothe any tension you're holding there.

Adding therapeutic Essential Oils to any of these routines increases the healthy benefits. There are many pre-made blends you can use for this purpose. Most contain some of the same Oils known to soothe sore, tired muscles and joints as well as calm the mind. Citrus Oils, Marjoram, Black Pepper, Neroli, and Wintergreen are all good choices. An easy way to make a good, basic massage blend for yourself is to combine Lavender and Peppermint Essential Oils with a carrier oil, like Fractionated Coconut Oil. Fractionated coconut is light, unscented, and doesn't stain your clothes. Massage therapists love it. If you want to make a little to use as you go, mix 3 drops of Lavender and two drops of Peppermint Essential Oil in the palm of your hand with a squeeze of Fractionated Coconut Oil. Rub your palms together, then massage the area needed. Remember to wash your hands after. If you happen to rub your eye with a little Peppermint left on your finger, you'll feel it!

**If essential oils get into the eye, dilute the area immediately with vegetable (olive, coconut, etc.) or other carrier oil. Do this by placing the vegetable oil on a tissue and gently dabbing at the eye area. Repeat as necessary.*

ESSENTIAL TAKE CARE TIP

#10 Make Time For Tea Time

Studies continue to show that drinking hot tea can help your body and brain in many ways. Tea – especially black, green and red-bush tea – contains natural anti-oxidants that can help boost your immune system and metabolism, calm your brain, and even help your bone and skin quality.

Research is still being done to figure out exactly how much you need to drink to get the most benefits, but for now, many experts suggest two cups a day. For the healthiest cup, choose lower or caffeine-free varieties, (I like chamomile) and lay off the sugar.

You can add Essential Oils to your tea to provide calming benefits. Before you do though, make sure to read the label and consult the manufacturer with any questions about guidelines for internal use. If it doesn't say that specifically, do not ingest it! Even when you are using a quality of Oil that is approved for internal use, it's important to remember that Essential Oils are highly concentrated, and the Oil version is much more potent than a herbal form…so don't overdo it! A little bit is all you need. Before adding my hot water and tea, I like to add a teaspoon of honey to the bottom of a cup, and then I just dip a toothpick in my bottle of Oil and swirl it in the honey—so I don't even use a full drop.

Here are some favorite Essential Oils to use in tea to help with relaxation:

- Lavender
- Roman Chamomile
- Bergamot
- Frankincense

ESSENTIAL TAKE CARE TIP

#11 Balance Your Brain

When you're having a tough time figuring out a solution to a problem, you need to summon the super power of both sides of your brain. That's not easy to do when you're feeling stressed or in a stressful situation. My friend, health psychologist Dr. Nancy Mramor, offers this little trick: Sit quietly, with your feet flat on the floor. Close your eyes, and take a few deep breaths in and out. Next, move your hands together and lightly bring the tips of your fingers together...try barely touching fingertips (eyes still closed). Feel the energy.

Dr. Mramor says this action works to balance your brain, bringing the strengths from left and right brain together to give you the mental blast you need to work your way through any trouble.

Frankincense is a beautiful Essential Oil to help support bringing balance to the brain. Just breathing a drop in from your hands or placing a drop on the crown of your head works wonders!

ESSENTIAL TAKE CARE TIP

#12 Prevent Head Tension

I know a man named Tasso Spanos, who has a Center for Pain Treatment on Pittsburgh's South Side. He specializes in a practice called Trigger Point Myotherapy. He applies pressure to certain trigger points, and teaches people how to do light stretches to focus on specific muscles that are the source of pain.

Tasso tells me that the #1 reported pain is the tension headache. The muscles responsible for causing tension headache pain are actually in the back of our neck, down the shoulder blades, and across the upper back. If you placed a coat hanger with the hook at the base of your neck on your back, it would outline the muscles I'm talking about.

Tasso says to prevent tension headaches you need to keep those muscles relaxed. Here's an easy stretch to help you with that:

1. Bend your elbows and place your palms together, finger tips up, as in prayer position.

2. Keeping your palms together, and as much as possible, your elbows together, slowly push your hands and arms straight up over your head. At the top, separate your palms, stretch each hand out to each side and bring them around to meet in the middle again at chest level, in prayer position.

Repeat this for a few minutes daily, or as many times a week as possible, whenever you happen to think about it. Please visit www.TakeCareTips.com to watch a short video demonstration of this technique!

Rubbing a pre-made Essential Oil massage blend that includes Cypress, Peppermint, Marjoram, Basil, Grapefruit and Lavender (or making your own by adding a couple of drops of any one or two of those to Fractionated Coconut Oil) into the back of the neck and tops of the shoulders helps to keep those muscles nice and loose, too.

ESSENTIAL TAKE CARE TIP

#13 Work It Off

Stress relief is one of the many benefits of regular activity. There's a whole chapter on exercise in this book for you (Chapter 3), but the positive, healthy aspects of simply moving more spill out into several other chapters.

Exercise helps with stress relief because it triggers the release of feel-good chemicals in your brain (let's hear it for endorphins!), and it happens fast! All it takes is a few seconds of activity to start to feel the effects. So, GET UP and get moving! Take a break and walk the dog. Chase the kids around the back yard. Grab some light weights (or water bottles, or soup cans) and do a little arm work. Jump on the bed. You're an adult now and no one can tell you not to.

It won't take long to feel that stress slip away. If you need a little energy boost to get started, good old Peppermint Essential Oil is great for that! Simply add a drop to your palm, rub your palms together, cup your hands over your nose and mouth (keeping your hands down, away from your eyes), and breathe in that invigorating scent! I will never tire of watching someone do that for the first time! The eyebrows go up, and most often they let out a "Whooooo!!"

ESSENTIAL TAKE CARE TIP

#14 Find Strength In Numbers

Going it alone is no fun, especially when you're trying to navigate through a stressful situation. You may feel like you "have to handle it yourself", but there's really no need to feel that everything must rest on your shoulders alone. Relieve some of the pressure by sharing some of the responsibility with other family members, or close trusted friends. Take a few minutes to confide in someone you feel comfortable with. Let them know you're having a tough time coping with everything, and that you could really use some time for yourself. If you're caring for someone in your home, or you just need someone to sit with the kids, ask that person if they could come and hold down the fort for even an hour. A change of scenery will do wonders for you, and by letting someone else in, you're creating a long-term support network. At first they might be surprised, since you've always seemed so on top of everything, but chances are very good that this person will say yes, and will continue to check up on you, without your even having to ask. It will be wonderful not to feel so alone.

If you need help with mustering up the courage to have that conversation, or with finding the right words, reach for Lavender Essential Oil. Such a gentle, but powerful Oil, Lavender is calming for the body and the brain. On an emotional level, it helps to soothe any fears of letting our true thoughts and feelings be heard. Honest communication is so important to our wellbeing. Rub a drop of Lavender over your heart and/or on the back of your neck and wrists for this kind of support.

ESSENTIAL TAKE CARE TIP

#15 Pet Power

Cute and cuddly creatures can calm your nerves! There's a whole practice around this idea called Pet Therapy. I know a woman who takes dogs into nursing homes and hospices. Her face lights up when she tells me about seeing all the smiles when she and her dogs walk into a room. Pets provide us with unconditional love and acceptance. A University of California, Los Angeles study I read found that the people they surveyed who owned a dog needed much less medical care for stress-related issues than those who did not own a dog. Even those confined to a bed can experience calm feelings by being able to glance over to watch a tank of colorful, swimming fish.

If you don't want to take on the responsibility of owning a pet, you can still get the therapeutic benefits by "borrowing" a neighbor's (most dog owners would be happy to have someone else walk the dog every once in a while), or volunteering a little time at an animal shelter.

And guess what? As you're using your Lavender to help you stay calm, it will work for your dog, too! In an episode of "The Dog Whisperer", renowned dog behavior expert Cesar Millan used a blend of Essential Oils that includes Lavender to help a dog relax and overcome fear. He let the dog smell the Oils from his hands, then rubbed his hands through the dog's fur.

Find more information about how to use Essential Oils safely with pets at www.TakeCareTips.com.

This really is one of my favorite tips in the book. As healthy-living as I like to preach, I love my chocolate! Imagine my joy when the news first came out about the health benefits of chocolate…was I dreaming? No! Chocolate, especially high quality dark chocolate, has the ability to relieve stress because of a chemical reaction that causes the brain to release those same happy brain hormones (endorphins again) that are released during exercise!

Sadly, this is not a prescription to eat a lot of chocolate. Just a small square does the trick. Thoroughly enjoy it by eating it like the French do: place it on your tongue, close your mouth, and let it melt there. Don't eat, read email or watch TV – be still and quiet for a moment. Just you and your wonderful piece of chocolate. I learned that fine chocolate eating method from Dr. Will Clower, author of *The Fat Fallacy* and *The French Don't Diet Plan*.

Here's a way to bump up the health benefits of chocolate, with Wild Orange Essential Oil, which provides a happy mood boost! This delicious recipe comes to us from Tenina Holder, a long-time Oils user and popular best-selling cookbook author in Australia, who believes chocolate is a health food. You'll hear more about her and get more Oil-infused recipes in Chapter 4.

RASPBERRY AND WILD ORANGE GANACHE TRUFFLES

Ingredients

10 Wild Orange Essential Oil

4 oz pure raspberry puree (no seeds, see note)

1 oz caster sugar

2 tsp vanilla bean paste

11 oz 54% chocolate in callets or in small pieces

1 tbsp unsalted butter

A few dried apricots

COATING

11 oz dark chocolate to coat

Edible red glitter to garnish (optional)

Method

Cook puree, sugar and vanilla on a medium low heat until thickened and fragrant. (Just bring to the boil, but do not boil.)

Add chocolate and melt slowly over low heat.

Add butter in pieces and combine briskly with a balloon whisk. Press out any unmelted butter with your spatula. Add Wild Orange Oil and stir to combine.

Scrape into a plastic container and allow to set at room temperature. Place in the fridge until you are ready to dip and roll truffles. Divide the mixture into even sized pieces and roll into balls. Refrigerate until quite solid. At least an hour.

Melt coating chocolate and roll truffles, garnishing as you go with the glitter. Allow to set.

TIP

Raspberry Puree can be purchased in frozen format from many sources. If you are struggling to find it, you can make it yourself from frozen raspberries.

Simply cook the raspberries until hot, press through a fine sieve to remove seeds. Reserve the remaining puree and weigh as needed for this recipe.

ESSENTIAL TAKE CARE TIP

#17 Tune It Out

Listen to your favorite soothing playlist. Have fun making a modern version of a mix tape…there's magic in those melodies! Music therapy is practiced everywhere and gets great results with autistic children, chronically and critically ill people, and victims of abuse. It can work for you, too. Research shows that music has therapeutic qualities related to stress relief and mood improvement. This is why spas and upscale restaurants have it piped in. Professional therapists are helping people with the music and Oils combination, too. Many diffuse Essential Oils during group and private sessions to help with relaxation. Here are some of the common diffuser blends they use. Choose the combinations you like from the recommended Oils:

RELAXING BLENDS

Ingredients

3	Lavender or Lemon **Essential Oil**
2	Bergamot, Clary Sage or Ylang Ylang **Essential Oil**
3	Lavender or Eucalyptus **Essential Oil**

Method

Following the manufacturer's instructions that came with your diffuser, fill your diffuser with water, then add the drops of Oils. Turn on the mist to create a space that supports relaxation.

Remember a diffuser allows you to scent your environment without the toxic ingredients in most sprays, candles, wax melts, and plug in scent packs.

Find more Essential Take Care Tips Diffuser Blend Recipes at www.TakeCareTips.com.

ESSENTIAL TAKE CARE TIP

#18 Slow Down

In today's world, it's easy to feel like we need to be expert multi-taskers. We get used to running around doing many things at once. If you stop for a minute and look around, you might realize that not everybody moves that way all the time. It's OK to slow down and focus on just one thing! In fact, it's much healthier to let some things go.

Take a few minutes to pare down your To Do list. Prioritize what's left and focus on crossing off one thing at a time. It does wonders for your morale and self-worth to check off completed tasks, and be able to reflect on all you've achieved!

> *Slow down and enjoy life. It's not only the scenery you miss by going too fast – you also miss the sense of where you are going and why.*
>
> -Eddie Cantor

While you're at it, allow yourself a couple of minutes to reflect on everything that you are accomplishing. All too often, the successes get lost in the midst of everything else there is to do. Don't let that happen. Stopping briefly to feel some pride in what you do will help you feel confident and balanced throughout the day. Here's a rollerball blend you can make that feels like a pat on the back for a job well done.

'ATTA GIRL BLEND

Ingredients

6 **Bergamot Essential Oil**
Turns innocence into joyfulness and reconnects individual with their heart

4 **Patchouli Essential Oil**
Encourages emotional honesty, love and forgiveness and honesty of heart

2 **Eucalyptus Essential Oil**
Supports self acceptance, awakens the soul to hope and cheerfulness

2 **Black Pepper Essential Oil**
Self understanding, fuels motivation and high energy

1 **Thyme Essential Oil**
Supports forgiveness, and an openness to love

Fractionated Coconut Oil

10ml Rollerball Bottle

Method

Add all the Essential Oils to the rollerball bottle. Fill the rest of the way with Fractionated Coconut Oil, and replace the rollerball. Roll on wrists, inside of elbows, behind the neck, or behind the ears to enjoy the benefits. This one smells so good, you may find yourself using it as a natural perfume, and that's OK!

ESSENTIAL TAKE CARE TIP

#19 Laugh It Up

You might not remember the last time you let loose with a really good laugh. Now would be a great time to try to get that back. Read a few pages from a funny book, watch a little bit of a funny TV show, or call a funny friend and tell her to give you her best stuff. YouTube is filled with thousands of videos that will have you howling (just be careful of falling into a YouTube black hole and losing the whole afternoon). The real impact of this isn't even funny: laughing, even just smiling, actually helps to reduce stress hormone levels. Medical research shows laughter works better than pharmaceuticals for depression and pain, affects the body like exercise, improves our blood flow, strengthens our immune system, regulates our blood sugar levels, and helps with better relaxation and sleep!

Let something funny take you away from your troubles for a bit and give you a quick burst of happy energy. Maybe it really is the best medicine.

You'd better not be smiling. Stop smiling! Stop it right now! Did that work? I used to get my kids with that quite a bit…thought it couldn't hurt to try.

Like we talked about in the Introduction, just breathing in Essential Oils can help to improve your mood. Citrus Oils and mints are often used to support happy energy.

HAPPY ENERGY DIFFUSER BLEND

Ingredients		Method
3	Grapefruit Essential Oil	Following the manufacturer's instructions, fill your diffuser with water, add the drops of Essential Oils, and turn it on to experience the benefits.
2	Peppermint Essential Oil	
1	Spearmint Essential Oil	

ESSENTIAL TAKE CARE TIP

#20 Just Say No

This is one of the hardest tips for me to follow.

"Can you have that presentation done by Thursday?" "Yep!" "Can you help me finish my project this afternoon?" "Absolutely!" "Can you bake 30 cupcakes for the class party on Tuesday?" "Of course, no problem."

Saying "No" is not one of my strengths. I like to help people. I want to help people. Too many of us do that at our own expense though, and that's not good. It's really the whole premise for this book: we allow the work that we do for others to take up so much of our time that we don't have any time left for ourselves. Running from one thing to the next with no downtime is extremely stressful. Sometimes I wonder if the running back and forth is harder than the actual tasks we have to do. We need to develop some personal limits and to stick to them. That means you're going to have to refuse some requests of your time. I heard this quote once, and it really stuck with me: "Saying YES to something means saying NO to something else." We only have so much time---we need to be better guardians of it! Take a few minutes and think about how you will respond when you are asked to do something that you don't have the time to do (or you just don't really want to do – it's OK to feel this way sometimes).

Sometimes having a script is all you really need to get you through it. How about "I'm sorry I just can't this time, I have a family commitment." Or what about the plain old truth, "I'm sorry, but I've been doing so much lately, Tuesday afternoon is a precious bit of time I carved out for myself, and I really have to stick to that." Who could argue with that? You're not hurting anyone's feelings like this, and you're not shutting yourself off from providing help in the future; you're just being a good manager of your time.

Tea Tree Essential Oil helps to support you as you stand firm with holding time for yourself. To feel the benefits, apply a drop around your belly button, or on the bottom of each foot.

CHAPTER
THREE

When you were little you didn't worry about creating an exercise program to stay fit. When you weren't in school, you woke up with the sunshine, ate breakfast, and then ran outside to play. Your mom would see you when she called you in for lunch and then again for dinner; and you'd come in for good when the street lights came on. You were doing what came naturally. You didn't think about tracking how many calories you were burning playing kick ball, you were just having FUN.

Your body still wants to move like that, but now you're grown up. The world has grown up, too. Technological advancements have made it so we don't have to walk down the street to say hello to a friend. In fact, we don't even have to speak! We can just text a "Hi, how ya doin'?"

The more that machines move and our muscles don't, the more we're hurting our bodies by not allowing them to do what they were meant to do. Our bodies were made for motion...but...we sit...a lot! I heard a doctor on a podcast describe sitting as "the new smoking" in terms of the threat it poses to our health!

It's easy to fool ourselves into thinking that we have been more active than we actually have. "Whew, what a busy day," we say. We feel drained, and we are drained---mentally, even emotionally---but physically we may not have done much of anything. We sit and keep up with relationships, run our businesses, pay our bills, and keep our lives in order as we click on our computers or phones. We wonder why our hips are sore. We wonder why our shoulders hurt. We wonder why we have headaches. "It must be this chair!" we think, and we buy fancy ergonomic office chairs to make us more comfortable. We buy more pillows for the couch. You know what would make us more comfortable? Getting up off our butts and moving around!

Our bodies crave motion, and will respond quickly when we start getting active. Now, if you haven't done any kind of exercising in a while, please talk with your doctor about what is OK for you to do. You certainly don't want to do too much too fast and hurt yourself. You don't need any more stress in your life. Don't rush these tips. Take your time with them. Enjoy the way that moving your body feels. Allow yourself to appreciate your new strength.

Scientists have spent centuries analyzing the mechanics of the human body, and exactly like a machine, our joints were created with motion in mind. When we don't move, we get rusty; and we're more likely to put on weight – which in turn puts us at a higher risk for a number of serious illnesses including heart disease, diabetes, some cancers, and asthma. I gave you statistics in Chapter 1 that showed you how a lack of self-care increases your risk of serious illness. It's scary, and it's real...but you have the power to turn things around.

I understand that, "Let's start an exercise program!" might feel like crazy-talk to someone who is burning the candle at both ends; but listen, we're not training for the Olympics here (although we'll get some motivation from someone who is!); we're not preparing for a call from Sports Illustrated for the next Swimsuit Edition. All we want to do is feel better and be healthier.

You can absolutely do that by using the fitness tips in this chapter. My goal with providing these tips is to show you that you don't need flashing neon lights and glitter to announce that you are going to start (cymbal crash, please) An Exercise Program. Working out doesn't have to be flashy or overwhelming, or expensive. It can be easy, and yes…even fun!

I love what a doctor I know told me about how he breaks through to the patients who tell him "I don't have enough time for exercise."

"Give me 30 minutes a day," he tells them. "Oh, I could never spare 30 minutes," they answer. "Then give me three 10-minute chunks, or six 5-minute chunks, or ten 3-minute chunks, or thirty 1-minute chunks!" he tells them. What the doctor's doing is helping people to break down that "big, scary" 30 minute number into little manageable pieces.

When we're looking for help (you've shown you're ready by buying this book), as much as we don't like to admit it, sometimes we just want to be told what to do. So, at the risk of sounding bossy, in this Chapter, I'm going to tell you exactly what to do. I'll give you little plans that you can follow to start building --even looking forward to---regular activity in your day. If you are caring for people who can join in the activity with you, it would be wonderful to include them whenever possible.

CAN 10 MINUTES OF EXERCISE REALLY HELP?

YES! One 10-minute tip alone is not an exercise program; but one 10-minute tip will start you on your way---and the most important thing you can do is to get started. Ten minutes of activity is much better than no minutes of activity. Keep reading to find out about some big positive things that will happen in 10 little minutes…

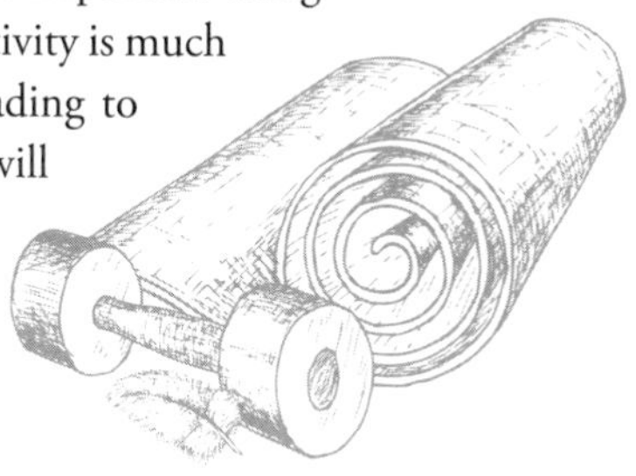

WHAT'S SO SPECIAL ABOUT 10?

Working in a newsroom for all of those years, I did hundreds of reports on the latest, greatest fitness fads, trends, and studies. Even for someone like me, with experience sorting through statistics, it was easy to get confused because of conflicting information. Just how much of what type of exercise is 100%-without- a- doubt- the- best? Recent research consistently proves that there are benefits to short spurts of exercise---and---ten seems to be the magic number:

- Psychologists at Northern Arizona University in Flagstaff found that 10 minutes of exercise improved mood, increased energy, and encouraged mental alertness and clarity. Interestingly, more than 10 minutes didn't bring about any new benefits related to mood.
- Researchers at the Pennington Biomedical Research Center at Louisiana State University found that 10 minutes of activity a day can provide immediate benefits, especially with heart health, and especially for people who haven't been doing much exercise at all.
- A study in the journal Plos One also found that "more" isn't necessarily "better" when it comes to exercise. It tracked three groups of sedentary people for 12 weeks. The first group did a 50-minute workout, the second group was allowed to do whatever they normally do to exercise, and the third group did three 10-minute workouts throughout the day. All workouts were monitored three days a week for the 12 weeks, and at the end, measures of insulin sensitivity, oxygen consumption and muscle function all improved about the same amount for people in both of the exercise groups. People in the group that didn't change anything didn't show any improvement. Those involved in the study described the results as good news for those who feel that time is a barrier to getting a beneficial workout.

HERE'S WHY:

Medical studies continue to prove major health benefits in ten minute workouts: improved heart health, brain function, happier mood, more energy, better skin, better sleep, and increased self-esteem! Plus, by working activity into your day in smaller chunks of time, you won't burn out.

After just a few 10-minute sessions, you'll notice that you're not so creaky when you get up out of a chair. Keep it up and you'll start to feel firmer. Your clothes will get a little loose. Others will notice and give you compliments and that's going to help you feel better about yourself, and keep on going.

Also, as you may know, getting physical can also help with getting physical with your partner. The positive mental and physical benefits you will feel from regular exercise can help a great deal with intimacy, which is another important component of overall wellness.

BUT WAIT, THERE'S MORE...MUCH MORE!

Exercise will boost your immune system, making you less susceptible to picking up every bug you may be exposed to at work, or spending time in your daughter's preschool. Regular activity is going to help you prevent or control high blood pressure and encourage healthy cholesterol levels. Exercise boosts good cholesterol and breaks down bad cholesterol to reduce the potential for plaque build-up that could block your arteries. Research has shown that exercise is just as effective as medicine in managing or preventing Type 2 diabetes. Being active will help to strengthen your lungs by moving oxygen and important nutrients to lung tissues.

Moving more during the day will also help you to have a deeper, more restful sleep at night. I will give you more details about the importance of quality sleep (and tips for how to get it) in Chapter 5, but for right now, know that when you sleep better your body is going to be able to function better all the way around.

The American Heart Association says it's important for us to get at least 30 minutes of activity five days a week; and recent studies show that three 10-minute blocks of activity are just as good as one 30-minute session! So, if you don't feel like you can find a half an hour for exercise, can you find 10 minutes? Of course you can.

Even if you've heard this information before, I'd like to gently point out that there's a big difference between knowing something and doing something. Sitting and thinking about exercise doesn't burn nearly as many calories, help your heart nearly as much, or make your muscles stronger, than actually getting up and exercising! Ten minutes can make a big difference in how you look and feel! Try it and see.

ESSENTIAL TAKE CARE TIP

#21 Make A Date With Yourself

Give yourself ten minutes to look at your schedule for the week and block out at least ten minutes for you to be active each and every day. I do this on Sunday nights. Start by going over what's already in your routine, and see how you can change some of your passive time to active time. Can you walk somewhere instead of driving? Can you replace a coffee break with a walk up and down the stairs where you work? Can you walk while you talk on a business call?

Then look at the time that's left. When you find a 10-minute chunk of time you can repossess, lock it in – in ink, so there's no going back. Ideally you want to aim for three 10-minute activity times most days of the week, but one or two is better than nothing! When you give yourself ten minutes to block out your 10 minute exercise dates, you'll see it can be done. Keep these appointments with yourself just as you would an appointment with anyone else.

Here's a DIY Essential Oil blend you can make to help you get into action:

I CAN DO THIS BLEND

Ingredients

2 Grapefruit Essential Oil

2 Lime Essential Oil

2 Peppermint Essential Oil

Fractionated Coconut Oil (optional)

10ml Rollerball Bottle (optional)

Method

Following the instructions that came with your diffuser, add Oils, and turn it on to experience the benefits. Using a combination of citrus and mint aromatically or topically will give you an instant happy energy boost! It is advised, due to photosensitivity, not to expose the area of skin that citrus Oils have been applied to, to the sun for at least 12 hours after application.

For a rollerball blend, add 5 drops of each Oil to an empty rollerball bottle. Fill the rest of the way with Fractionated Coconut Oil, replace the rollerball and roll on pulse points.

ESSENTIAL TAKE CARE TIP

#22 Just Walk

As you know, one of the best things you can do to lose weight or feel more energized is to move more. One of the easiest ways to move more is simply to walk! It's safe, it's easy, and it's FREE. My friend, and fitness expert, Leslie Sansone is the creator of Walk at Home, the #1 in-home walking program in the world. It allows you to walk along with the Your Daily Walk app, a variety of DVD's or digital video workouts, or in fun group fitness classes with the new Walk 15 program, and get in a one, two, or even a five mile walk by following along with four basic steps that keep you moving at the speed you need for serious results. Millions of people have lost weight and added years to their lives with Leslie's workouts. I myself lost 18 pounds in six weeks with Leslie's DVD's after the birth of my fifth child. The flexibility of the program is what got me to try it. I didn't have to leave the house. I did many of the workouts in my pj's, with my toddlers moving right along with me! It worked!

Here's a 10-Minute Walking Workout plan from Leslie that will help you maximize your exercise time:

Walk slowly to warm up for 1 minute.

Pick up the pace a little bit for 2 minutes.

Get moving to a brisk pace for 5 minutes, pump those arms!

Gradually slow back down, but keep moving for 2 minutes.

If you are able to take this outside, by all means go for it! The fresh air and sunshine will do you good. If you need to stay inside, switch the walk to a march, add some upbeat music to keep your pace, and you can work out in a very small area.

AND WHEN YOU'RE READY FOR MORE...

When you get the 10-minute walk down, try to fit in two more during the day. Together, those sessions will be just as effective as one 30-minute walk. You can increase the intensity by walking with some one or two pound hand weights, or add a little bit of jogging into your walk. You can find some of the Walk at Home and Walk 15 workouts at www.TakeCareTips.com.

Before, during, and after a workout, it's important to stay hydrated. I have more about that for you in our chapter on nutrition. But for now, know that drinking water will fuel your body to be able to perform well during the work out, and help you recover and re-energize after.

Adding Essential Oils to your water gives you extra physical and emotional benefits...plus…if you're one of those people who "doesn't like water" you'll love the added flavor! Now as we've talked about a few times in this book already, you've got to be a smart consumer of Essential Oils. Make sure to read the labels, and even call the company if you need to, so that you're sure the Oils you have are safe for internal use. It's extremely important to take great care with making sure your Oils are safe, 100% pure, and non-toxic. It's also important to understand that Essential Oils are very potent, and one drop goes a long way. One drop in the water you drink 2 or three times a day is a good, safe way to get started. (I have more information about the Oils I use and trust at www.TakeCareTips.com.) Once you're sure of that, think of the flavors you can create! Here are some of the basics that are known for cleansing and purifying, providing energy, immune support, and metabolic support:

- Lemon
- Lime
- Wild Orange
- Grapefruit
- Peppermint
- Spearmint

To use, just add one drop to your water, and drink. Make sure to use a glass or aluminum water bottle, and if you use a straw, that should be glass, steel or aluminum, too.

ESSENTIAL TAKE CARE TIP

#23 Stand And Stretch

For those of you who acknowledge that you're getting older, (I like to stay in denial), you may notice your range of motion decreasing. Maybe just putting your socks on, or zipping up your dress is more of a production than it used to be. An easy way to improve in this area is simply taking a few minutes every day to stretch.

Stretching relieves muscle and mental tension, improves flexibility and coordination, and increases circulation. Regular stretching will help prevent injuries and make it easier for you to do all of the things you need to do during your day, because it lengthens your tendons, allowing your muscles to move the way you need them to. Stretching feels good, too. Your body loves it! It's easy, yet energizing.

An app called StretchIt quotes celebrities like Oprah, Serena Williams, Madonna, Beyoncé, and more who credit stretching with increased overall wellness.

Do some gentle neck rolls, stretch from side to side. Bend down and try to touch your toes. Reach up high all the way through your fingertips. Aim to get a nice full extension of your muscles.

No matter which muscles you want to focus on, do it safely by stretching slowly and smoothly – no bouncing or locking joints, as this only increases stress and muscle tightness. Also, it's very important to keep breathing as you stretch. Nice deep breaths, in through the nose and out through the mouth, will help let go of tension and increase the range of your stretch.

You can easily fit a few minutes of stretching into most days, whether you're sitting, standing, or lying down. Take advantage of a few minutes even before you get out of bed in the morning, and before you go to bed at night.

To deepen the relaxing effects of stretching, get into a soothing bath with an Essential Oil infused Epsom Salt soak. Did you know Epsom Salt isn't actually salt at all? It's a naturally occurring pure mineral compound of magnesium and sulfate. Noted benefits include soothing sore muscles, calming skin conditions, and improving quality of sleep.

EPSOM SALT
soak

EASY ESSENTIAL EPSOM SALT SOAK

Ingredients

5 Lavender Essential Oil

5 Peppermint Essential Oil

1 cup Epsom salts

Mason jar for storage

Method

In a large bowl, add Lavender and Peppermint Essential Oils to Epsom Salt and stir together. Transfer to Mason jar to store. Add 1/4 to 1/2 cup to a warm bath and soak for 10-20 minutes.

ESSENTIAL TAKE CARE TIP

#24 Sound The Alarm

Set the alarm on your phone, or your computer to go off every hour or two. When you hear the alarm, get up and stretch, walk around a bit, just do something to get your body moving. It's so easy to lose track of time when you're caring for others, and that little alarm will alert you to stop and spend a few minutes on yourself. If you're with someone when it goes off, it creates an opportunity for a nice little conversation about WHY it happened, and what it means to you. Whoever you're with will most likely show you some support, and that will be great for your mindset! You also may inspire others to get healthier…wouldn't that feel awesome?!

Speaking of inspiration, I'd like to introduce you to a Dutch-Ghanaian Olympic athlete named Akwasi Frimpong. He's a sprinter, bobsledder, and skeleton athlete who has won four bronze, four silver, and eight gold medals in national and international sporting events. His 2018 appearance in the Winter Olympics was not medal-winning, but he celebrated his accomplishments, and quickly turned to set his sights on winning a medal in the 2020 Olympic Games.

As someone who's dealt with, what others may consider "setbacks" throughout his life, Akwasi embraces the experiences as a needed part of the journey, and actually welcomes them!

"If failure was the only last step, there wouldn't be something called success," he says. What a beautiful mindset. Make yourself a priority---and do the best you can with that every day.

Akwasi is a dōTERRA performance athlete, and uses Essential Oils at home with his family, saying, "The fact that I can have these natural things in little bottles and take them everywhere I go, is a huge blessing."

Here are some of his favorites:

- Peppermint Essential Oil: "I put a little bit of Peppermint in my helmet before sliding for alertness and focus while going 70/80 miles per hour, head first, with my chin three inches from the ice."
- Deep Blue® Rub: "It's my number one go-to before or after workouts. I also use it to get fired up before competitions."
- dōTERRA On Guard® "I will put drops of dōTERRA On Guard® in my water bottle or in a capsule, and I use the dōTERRA On Guard® Toothpaste to brush my teeth every morning."
- dōTERRA Lifelong Vitality Pack®: "I don't travel without this. I take two pills of each bottle in the morning after breakfast and at night after dinner. The dōTERRA Lifelong Vitality Pack has really boosted my immune system*." (The Lifelong Vitality Pack® is a set of three supplements formulated to provide essential nutrients, metabolism benefits, and powerful antioxidants for energy and health.) Find out more about these products at www. TakeCareTips.com.

ESSENTIAL TAKE CARE TIP

#25 Fast Firming

A total body gym that you can fit in your pocket or purse? Yes! Have you ever used a Fitness Band? It's a long, narrow, thin piece of latex that you can take with you as a secret metabolism booster to use anytime, anywhere. They're sometimes called Thera-Bands, or Resistance Bands.

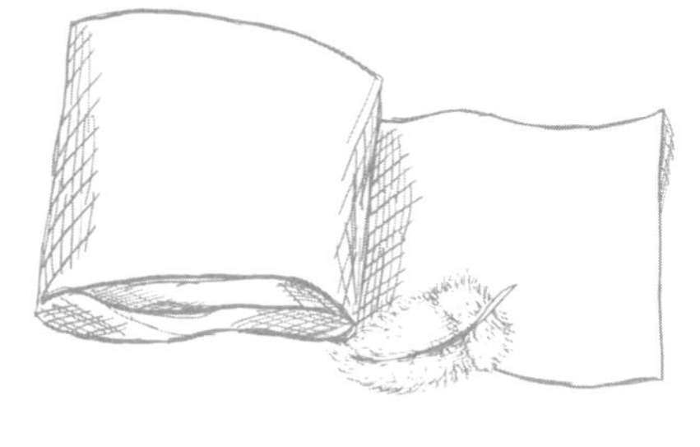

In ten minutes or less, you can work your whole body. For example, to work your arms, sit and anchor the band on the floor under your feet, then grab both sides and do bicep curls, keeping your elbows close to your sides and bending and raising them up, and then slowly letting them back down—holding on to the band the whole time. Repeat.

You can work your chest by holding the fitness band out in front of you, arms extended and shoulder-width apart. Holding onto the band, stretch your arms out to the side, then bring them back in, and repeat. You can adjust the tension by moving your hands closer together or farther apart.

Registered Nurse Atiya Abdelmalik creates healthy lifestyle programs. She uses Fitness Bands for herself and encourages people to keep a band in their desk drawer, purse, or briefcase. You can sneak in some self-care by pulling out your Fitness Band and doing a few easy moves. Abdelmalik says, "As caregivers we go, and go, and go until our bodies break down and then we wonder how did we get here; not realizing that we've been on the journey to this place for a long time. To reverse the trend, do something for yourself even when you're feeling great. Don't wait for a crisis."

Boost all of this good metabolism support with Grapefruit Essential Oil. Grapefruit has been shown to help curb cravings, increase energy, and burn fat. Essential Oils alone will not magically make you 2 sizes smaller all by themselves, but they will be an effective support system during your fitness journey to help you maximize your results.

Just inhaling Grapefruit Essential Oil triggers an enzyme in your saliva that is known to build a healthy metabolism, boost endurance, and control fat---especially belly fat!

Diffusing a few drops of Grapefruit Essential Oil for 10 minutes three times a week will support appetite control. It is advised, due to photosensitivity, not to expose the area of the skin that citrus Oils have been applied to, for at least 12 hours after application. Go ahead and mix a couple of drops with Fractionated Coconut Oil and massage it in to your body to stimulate the lymphatic system to release toxins. People also love to add a couple of drops of Grapefruit to a natural dry brushing routine to help tighten and smooth the skin.

ESSENTIAL TAKE CARE TIP

#26 Get Strong

Strength Training is not only for members of the NFL. Simply put, strength training is doing exercises that push your muscles to work harder, so they grow stronger. A ten-minute strength training workout will get your metabolism going and keep your body burning fat for up to 24 hours! You don't always need weights to get these benefits…you can use your own body weight. Try to do three of these 3-step strength training sessions every week:

Step 1: Do as many lunges as you can in 1 minute. To do a basic front lunge, stand with your hands on your hips. Step out with one leg, and bend that front knee down low. Keep your feet planted and your back straight. Concentrate on your posture and take care not to bend your front knee to the point that it extends past your toes to avoid straining the knee or hip. Good form is important here. Your back should be perfectly perpendicular to the floor. The calf of your bent front leg should be too. From this position, drop your pelvis straight down, then bring yourself back up and repeat. Switch your legs, check your posture and repeat the lunges with the other leg in front.

Step 2: Do as many squats as you can in 1 minute. To do a basic squat, stand straight, shoulders relaxed, arms at your sides, feet shoulder width apart, knees slightly bent. Keeping your feet planted, push your bum out to the back and bend your knees like you're going to sit down in a low chair. You can rest your hands on your legs or clasp them straight out in front of you, whatever's most comfortable. Remember to breathe. Hold yourself in the squat for a couple of seconds, then come back up to the starting position. Repeat.

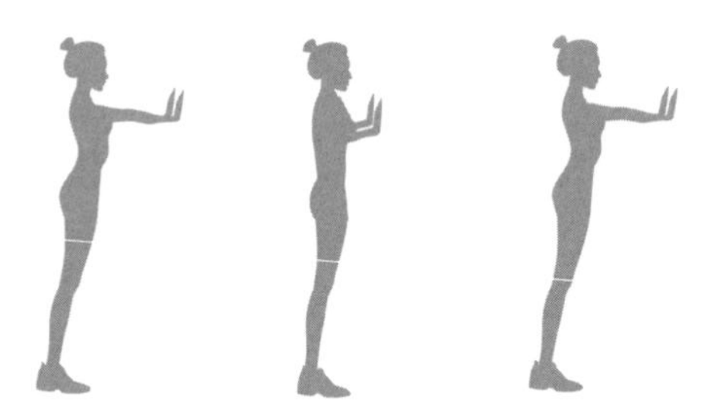

Step 3: Do as many standing push-ups as you can in 1 minute. To do a standing push-up, stand about three feet away from a wall, stretch your arms out to the front and place your palms on the wall at shoulder level, but a little wider than your shoulders. Keeping your feet planted, lean forward into the wall, letting your elbows bend out to the side, keeping your back straight. Move in to let your chest come close to the wall, but don't actually touch your chest to the wall. Then, press into your hands and arms and push yourself back up to a standing position. Repeat.

Rest for 30 seconds then repeat the three exercises. Rest again for 30 seconds and repeat the series one more time.

This is a more intense fitness tip, so remember to check with your doctor before trying it. Keep breathing through the moves and do only what you're comfortable with. You'll notice your strength increasing, and it'll feel great to add one more lunge or squat to your routine as you get stronger. Quality is more important than quantity with these exercises. Take care to pay attention to keeping good form throughout.

Add Essential Oils (keep reading for suggested recipe) to soothe sore muscles, and allow you to work on better range of motion and flexibility. You could use any one of these oils and it would help…or, combine them in your own blend to use as needed.

MUSCLE SOOTHER BLEND

Ingredients

3 Rosemary Essential Oil
Helps with circulation

4 Lavender Essential Oil
Anti-inflammatory, calming

3 Wintergreen Essential Oil
Acts as a numbing agent

2 Cinnamon Bark Essential Oil
Soothes and warms the muscles; reduces swelling

2 Vetiver Essential Oil
Increases blood flow, soothes the body and brain

3 Black Pepper Essential Oil
warming agent; also great to use before a workout

Fractionated Coconut Oil or other liquid Carrier Oil

10 ml Rollerball Bottle

Method

Add all the Essential Oils to the rollerball bottle. Fill the rest of the way with Fractionated Coconut Oil. Roll a little on areas needed and massage into the muscles before warm up or cool down stretching. Be careful to wash your hands after, so you don't accidentally get any in your eyes.

Massage is not just a luxury, it's a way to healthier, happier life.

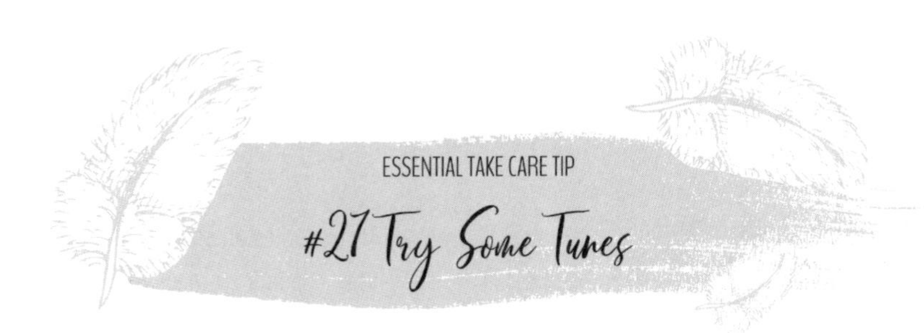

ESSENTIAL TAKE CARE TIP

#27 Try Some Tunes

The jury's still out about whether listening to music can actually affect your breathing and heart rate, but plenty of studies show that people who listen to music while they're going through their fitness programs are happier, more energetic, and feel better about the quality of their workout. The beat of the music helps to set your overall pace. Upbeat songs with consistent rhythms seem to work best. Lose yourself in some of your favorite music the next time you exercise and chances are you will feel motivated to work out longer and stronger!

If you don't just want background music, turn it up and dance for ten minutes! You may end up having so much fun, you forget that it counts as exercise. Think of all the weight-loss stories to come out of that Dancing with the Stars show. Dancing works your whole body, and it's an effective cardio workout, too.

Need help with energy to get up and move? Break out your Peppermint Essential Oil. Just breathing it in (from a diffuser, a drop in the palm of your hand, or straight from the bottle) will give you an instant lift.

ESSENTIAL TAKE CARE TIP

#28 Give A Shout Out

Call someone you are close with and tell them that you are now motivated to start taking better care of yourself by exercising. Tell this person exactly what you hope to accomplish, whether it's losing some weight or increasing your energy. In fact, make it a point to tell as many as you can about your fitness goals.

You are creating your own support network. Maybe the people around you have been hoping they could reach out and help you in some way; they'll be happy to help to monitor your progress and keep you on track. It's easy to let social life fade away while you're caring for others. Creating this network is a way for you to stay in touch. I'd love to have you join our Facebook support community, too! Find us here: **https://www.facebook.com/groups/TakeCareTipsCommunity/**

AND IF YOU'RE READY FOR MORE...

Block out some extra time to actually go out with the people in your support network. See this as an opportunity for some healthy multi-tasking, or just getting that important dose of friendship while getting fit. Run errands together. Do yard work or housework together, sign up for a charity walk together. The activity and interaction are both wonderful for your well-being.

ESSENTIAL TAKE CARE TIP

#29 Get On The Ball

Do you have trouble forming bonds? Many people who aren't taking care of themselves end up becoming disconnected from family and friends. The *Emotions and Essential Oils* book by Enlighten Healing says Cedarwood is the Oil of Community, and just breathing it in will help bring you together with people, and allow you to better receive the gift of love and support from others.

When patients at the Physical Medicine and Rehabilitation Division at Allegheny General Hospital in Pittsburgh ask the Director, Dr. Barbara Swan what the best exercise would be for them she always has the same answer: "The one you'll do."

Dr. Swan helps many people who deal with chronic pain by teaching them about the importance of self-care. "I try to make them understand that if they're not healthy, they can't do anything good for anyone else," she says"

Dr. Swan says you don't even need to find ten minutes to start a fitness program if you revamp your routine with more active versions of things you're already doing.

For example, when at your desk working, or sitting and visiting with a loved one you're caring for; replace the chair you're sitting in with a fitness ball. You know those big inflatable balls---sometimes called exercise balls, or stability balls. They were originally used for rehabilitation, but their versatility and effectiveness makes them a great fitness tool for anyone. If you've never tried a fitness ball before, you're in for a treat. It's fun. It's relaxing. You'll probably feel a little goofy the first time you're on it. You'll be a little wobbly; and that's why the fitness ball works so well. It forces you to use several different muscles at once to keep yourself balanced; so just sitting on the fitness ball and keeping yourself upright is a workout.

Sitting on a fitness ball strengthens your core muscles (all the muscles around your belly; front and back). When you have a strong core, your posture improves, your balance improves, and lifting and carrying become easier.

Keep in mind that the harder the ball is, the tougher the exercises will be, so don't over inflate the ball when you're starting out. Also, there are different sizes of fitness balls. You need to make sure to get the best one for you based on your height. Look for guidelines on the packaging.

AND WHEN YOU'RE READY FOR MORE...

There are hundreds of exercises you can do on a fitness ball to get all your muscles moving. Start by just playing around a little bit. As you move around, take the time to feel the different muscles that spring into action to keep you balanced.

Then try something a little more organized: from sitting, walk your feet forward. Lie back, and let the fitness ball support you. While comfortably lying on the ball with your feet flat on the floor about two feet away, stretch your arms out to the sides, then pull them into the center. Lower your arms back down to the sides, and repeat. You are doing an exercise called a chest fly and you can increase the intensity even more by holding light hand weights, or soup cans while you do the arm movements. Leg, ab, arm, and chest muscles all get some action with this exercise.

While you're balancing your body, why not work on balancing your mind as well? A pre-made Grounding Blend of Oils featuring Spruce Leaf, Ho Wood Leaf, Frankincense Resin, Blue Tansy Flower, Blue Chamomile Flower, and Osmanthus Flower supports a sense of harmony, and calm focus. Simply breathe it in, or apply a drop to the back of your neck, top of head, temples, forehead, wrists, or bottoms of feet to help ease anxious feelings.

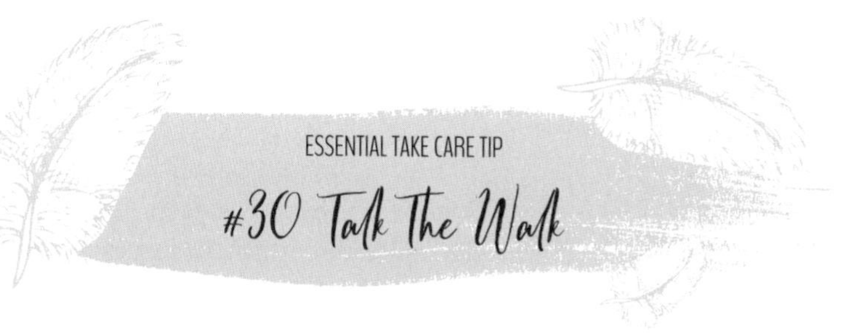

ESSENTIAL TAKE CARE TIP

#30 Talk The Walk

I got this tip from a woman who was in the audience at a Take Care Tips talk I gave at a Women's Conference. She is a caregiver to her husband who has Alzheimer's disease. Caring for him keeps her at home most of the time. She doesn't get out much to see family or friends, but she does try to keep in touch with them by setting times for weekly phone calls. She got the idea to use those phone calls as a reminder to get up and move. When the phone rings, she gets up and walks around the house while she talks! She stays moving for the whole conversation and she even started wearing a monitor to keep track of her movement. 2,000 steps equals about a mile, and the woman told me that she can sometimes get that in during one long conversation!

Enhance your mood with this happy blend from the *MyMakes : Nature's Medicine Cabinet for Home & Family:*

The cleansing, purifying and invigorating properties of Lemon contained in this blend (both physically and mentally) make it very versatile, but we have chosen this recipe to support a peaceful and focused mind, as well as provide uplifting and motivating benefits for the mind and body.

PEACEFUL PLACE ROLLER BLEND

Ingredients

4 Lemon Essential Oil

5 Bergamot Essential Oil

4 Wild Orange Essential Oil

1 Frankincense Essential Oil

1 Peppermint Essential Oil

Fractionated Coconut Oil or other liquid Carrier Oil

10 ml Rollerball Bottle

Method

Add Essential Oils to the roller bottle and top with carrier of your choice, we recommend Fractionated Coconut Oil. Roll the blend over the chest, heart and pulse points throughout the day as needed.

This blend contains a citrus Oil and it is advised not to expose any area of skin where the Oil has been applied to the sun for at least 12 hours after application, due to photosensitivity.

Get more recipes at www.TakeCareTips.com.

CHAPTER
FOUR

Get in here & eat

More than two thousand years ago, Hippocrates, the ancient Greek physician (known as the Father of Medicine) said, "Let thy food be thy medicine, and medicine be thy food."

Much more recently, your mother (known as Mom, Mum, or Mama) backed that up, perhaps not as eloquently, with "You're not leaving this table until you eat your vegetables!"

Not eating properly is one of the common fallouts from caregiving, and it's also one of the big reasons family caregivers are turning into patients themselves. Way too many of us have poor eating habits. It's an issue of quality and quantity. We're consuming more processed "food" than ever.

If you were a car and you put bad fuel-or no fuel-in your tank, you'd just sputter along and then grind to a halt. It's very much like that with your body. Not giving your body the fuel it needs-combined with stress, and lack of sleep and exercise- is a recipe for illness. I'd like to take a moment now to talk about how the nutrients in food act in your body. You'll see right away why eating well should be a priority for everyone, and especially for caregivers.

WHAT DO I NEED TO KNOW?

Our amazing bodies can do a lot for us if we keep them filled with the basics so that they can do their jobs. We have incredible high-tech systems built right in that can protect us from Alzheimer's disease, heart disease, many kinds of cancers, and other illnesses. Medical researchers are finding that substances in foods actually have the power to give important orders to our genes-orders that can relate to specific diseases.

For example, oleic acid in olive oil has been shown to stop an aggressive type of gene found in women with breast cancer. Nutrients in broccoli and cauliflower have been shown to switch on certain genes whose job it is to make us resistant to cancer in the digestive system. And all this is going on silently while you enjoy your olive oil and broccoli!

Eating a variety of foods and drinking enough water boosts our immune system, and increases our chances that our bodies will be able to prevent and, in some cases, cure diseases that may threaten us - no pills required!

We continue to hear a lot about antioxidants in food. Check out the packages you have in your fridge. Many probably boast "antioxidants!" on the label.

What the heck are antioxidants? They are substances found in fruits and vegetables, some vitamins and amino acids. They work to prevent and repair cell damage caused by the sun, smoking, and aging for example. And they don't stop there; antioxidants may also help to boost your immune system and decrease your risk of some cancers.

A nutritionist told me that the process works in the body sort of like how a piece of banana starts to brown after you cut it. Sprinkling on some lemon juice (containing Vitamin C, a powerful antioxidant) stops the browning/aging effect.

Lycopene is one of the most recent antioxidants to be discovered (scientists think there are probably many, many more still to be studied). Lycopene is what makes tomatoes (and grapefruit, and watermelon) red. It may help to lower the risk of prostate cancer, breast cancer, and cardiovascular disease, as well as a variety of other illnesses.

Bottom line: although many new scientific findings are opening our eyes to the infinitely complex ways that food supports the wondrous systems in our bodies, the old school lesson of balance, variety and moderation still holds true. That's the common-sense approach to thinking about nutrition.

SO, WHAT SHOULD I BE EATING?

In issuing a report on dietary guidelines, the US Department of Agriculture stated that the "major causes of morbidity and mortality in the United States are related to poor diet and a sedentary lifestyle."

We now know that we should be eating a variety of foods from basic groups including grains, fruits and vegetables, fats and dairy products. And we need to limit the amount of saturated and trans fats, cholesterol, added sugars, salt and alcohol in our diets.

Portion sizes are different for each of us. If you go to the Department of Agriculture's web site, www.ChooseMyPlate.Gov, you will get a customized food pyramid based on your age, sex, height, weight, and level of activity. The food pyramid gives you the kinds and amounts of food right for you, along with recipe ideas for how to get the nutrients you need.

EAT FOR ENERGY

Some substances in food can give us natural energy boosts, other substances in food can make us tired. Time to take a look at those.

If you're chronically tired, don't just assume that's just a normal part of being a caregiver. There could be more going on. Now, it might be tricky to figure out if you're tired because you haven't eaten well, or you haven't had enough sleep, or because you have been under a lot of stress-or maybe because you are a little sick.

If you believe you are otherwise healthy and you're noticing that you just don't have as much energy as you'd like, start by analyzing and playing around a bit with when you eat, and how much you eat:

- Six mini-meals instead of three larger ones throughout the day may be what your body needs to run at its best levels.
- Check your portions. Regularly eating too much can lead to weight gain, which will slow you down. Not eating enough could deprive your body of needed nutrients. Women, especially, can feel tired if they have low iron.
- Are you eating too many empty carbohydrates, like white bread and sugary snacks? This can spike your blood sugar and then cause it to crash, taking your energy with it. Try to eat more complex carbs, like whole grains or fruit. Even better, combine them with lean proteins, like tuna or cottage cheese, to stay energized longer.
- Are you drinking a lot of alcohol? It is a depressant.
- Are you drinking enough water? Dehydration can cause a lack of energy.
- Are you overweight? Extra weight is a big energy-zapper. Don't skip meals, but make sure to fill them with healthy foods, and get regular exercise (see Chapter 3).

Monitor what you're eating and drinking for a few days. If you feel like you're eating properly, but you still feel very tired, it would be good to visit your doctor to talk about your symptoms. Chronic fatigue can be a sign or symptom of many other things.

EAT FOR STRESS RELIEF

Our bodies and minds are simply able to cope better when we're getting all of the nutrients we need. A lot of traditional comfort food is notorious for its calorie and fat count, but has almost no nutritional value (and probably empty carbohydrates, too, so you crash after eating). There are plenty of things that you can eat to soothe your stress levels and boost your nutrition without adding the worry of weight gain to your troubles. Here are just some of them:

Berries: they're packed with vitamin C, which helps to keep the stress hormone cortisol at bay. And as a powerful antioxidant, berries help to protect and heal your body from the negative effects of stress.

Nuts: doesn't take a lot to do the trick. An ounce of walnuts, Brazil nuts, or almonds work to boost nutrients that can help fight stress-related cell damage in the body. Nuts are a good source of protein and heart-healthy fats, too. Almonds are also said to help lower blood pressure.

Avocados: loaded with B vitamins, potassium, and vitamin E, avocados help to keep you calm by replenishing these important nutrients to the brain and nerves. They're also a great source of –of course- avocado oil, which is one of the healthiest fats you can eat.

Oranges: your body doesn't make vitamin C by itself, and since stress can tear down our body's storage of vitamin C, we need to re-stock often. Vitamin C helps to strengthen our immune system.

Tuna: full of Omega-3 fatty acids, which help to regulate the hormone adrenaline (this works to give you fast energy boosts when needed). Choose white tuna packed in water for a low-fat way to enjoy the health benefits.

Spinach: contains high levels of the mineral magnesium, which helps the body and brain with several functions, including the ability to keep you naturally calm.

I'LL DRINK TO THAT!

As long as it's water, drink up! Two-thirds of our bodies are made up of water. It helps to regulate body temperature, promote good digestion, protect our joints, and power our energy levels.

Water is so critical to the body that if you aren't putting enough in, your body will start to divert all of its energy to resolving that issue, instead of working for you in all the other ways it can. Water is your body's prime chemical component. Making up about 60 percent of your body weight. Every cell, tissue, and organ in your body needs water to survive and thrive. Drinking water helps your body to eliminate waste, maintain a healthy temperature, and protect tissues and joints. Several studies have shown most of us walk around at least mildly dehydrated---that's a huge energy zapper, and can also cause pain.

There's a lot of talk about exactly how much water we need. The best answer to that question is that everyone needs a different amount, based on our weight, where we live, whether we're taking medications, and more.

The National Academies of Sciences, Engineering, and Medicine says that for people of average health who live in temperate climates, men need about 15 and a half cups of water a day, and women need 11 and a half.

Cups of water needed per day

MEN x 15.5

WOMEN x 11.5

Some of the water we get each day comes from the foods we eat (about 20%), the rest comes from what we drink. It's important to have extra water during exercise, as well as when taking some medications, or if you are on a high-fiber diet. Most importantly; don't wait until you're thirsty to replenish.

Have you ever forgotten to drink water? That may seem a little silly, but it happens…especially among caregivers and other busy people. We are so focused on taking care of other people and things that we actually forget about handling this basic need. I've caught myself carrying around a water bottle that's still full in the afternoon! Staying hydrated is so important that there are many popular water-tracker apps that not only help you easily log how much water you drink each day, but also can remind you to take a drink! Check them out and download one with features you like. There are several free and low-cost options.

FOOD AND FAMILY

I don't want all this nuts and bolts talk about your need for healthy food to take away from the simple fact that eating a meal together as a family can be a wonderful emotional experience---good for strengthening the spirit and solidifying family relationships!

My friend Pasquale Vericella is a chef to the stars, and the proud owner of his dream-come-true; Il Cielo, a restaurant voted The Most Romantic in Beverly Hills. To him, the restaurant represents the culmination of years of experience of his family's love of food and entertaining.

Pasquale grew up around a mother and grandma who worked magic in the family kitchen with what they grew in their garden. "I can't say enough about preparing meals with family and eating together," Pasquale told me. "The lasting impression of learning how to cook from your parents; remembering the scent of the kitchen and the family's special recipes, the stories they told about how their parents taught them to cook, and the funny things that they experienced- It goes on and on. And then one day, you become the grandparent. We live with our memories. Life is a gift, full of shared love and experiences that we hand down from generation to generation."

Pasquale's mother died of Alzheimer's disease in 2000. His parents had moved in with his brother's family when it became clear that she needed 24-hour care. During his mother's long decline, Pasquale and his family flew home several times to spend time with her-and with his father. "We cared for them with love and enjoyed every minute of her last days. Stress, sorrow, regret, anger – all of these feelings came with this disease called Alzheimer's," Pasquale told me. "The only way to cope with all of this is to realize you must stay healthy and love yourself the way your mother, in this case, loved you. "

As a person who believes that sharing good food can be a tangible expression of caring, Pasquale offers some from-the-heart advice. He believes that having a simple meal is a wonderful thing for a caregiver and the person they are caring for to enjoy together, because it turns into much more than a meal. "It's about sharing the normal experience of life with a person you are caring for, "Pasquale says. "Making them feel relevant and, with Alzheimer's, helping them to remember the good times, the normal times. Enjoy every little smile, give them hugs, touch their hand and don't forget to be funny! Eating together is important part of caregiving." Look for a delicious, fast recipe from Pasquale in the Tips section of this chapter.

WHERE DO ESSENTIAL OILS FIT IN?

Since ancient times, people have been using Essential Oils in recipes. Food grade Essential Oils (make sure to read labels!) open up a whole new world in the kitchen, providing scents and tastes that carry health benefits, too.

Ginger, for example supports healthy digestion. It's also known to be an anti-inflammatory, and provides antioxidant benefits.

Remember, when buying essential oils for internal use, make sure to purchase something that's been tested for purity, and contains no fillers, synthetic, or toxic ingredients. Read the label on the bottle, and please call the company with any questions or concerns.

When using Essential Oils in recipes, also keep in mind that they're highly concentrated. You'll only use 1-2 drops in many cases; in some, even less. Just a toothpick dipped in the Oil and swirled in the food is enough. Since the Oils are sensitive to high heat, it's also a good idea to add them at the end, before serving.

Here's a list of Essential Oils Certified as GRAS (Generally Regarded as Safe and Food Additives by the FDA):

- Basil
- Bergamot
- Cardamom
- Cassia
- Cinnamon Bark
- Clary Sage
- Clove
- Coriander
- Frankincense
- Geranium
- Ginger
- Grapefruit
- Lavender
- Lemon
- Lemongrass
- Lime
- Melissa
- Tea Tree
- Marjoram
- Myrrh
- Oregano
- Patchouli
- Peppermint
- Rosemary
- Sandalwood
- Thyme
- Vetiver
- White Fir
- Wild Orange
- Ylang Ylang

OK, I'M CONVINCED...HOW DO I START?

With Breakfast! Boy, that's an easy meal to skip, isn't it? However, research continues to support that eating breakfast helps keep your mind sharp, your weight in check, and your energy levels up.

A dietician I know suggests oatmeal with raisins, whole grain toast with peanut butter and an apple, or a toasted whole grain bagel topped with a slice of cheese. Quick and yummy.

Each of these choices include a carbohydrate and a protein that allow you to start the day with energy and endurance.

Here are some more 10-Minute Tips and recipes to help you keep your healthy nutrition habits going…all the way to the bedtime snack:

ESSENTIAL TAKE CARE TIP

#31 Create A Healthy Space

When you walk into your kitchen, do you feel happy because it's a clean fresh space that you know is easy to work in, and filled with healthy food choices? If not…wouldn't it be great to create that for the heart of your home? You can do it in 10-minute sessions if needed!

Diffuse 2 drops of Rosemary and 3 drops of Lemon to clear the air, keep your mood bright, and help you stay focused while you do this work. Set the timer for 10 minutes and…

- Attack the fridge: Moving quickly, take everything out and check the dates. Ask yourself if it's something you'll use, and if it fits in with the healthier way of eating you want.
- Move through the pantry: Set your timer again, and go through what you're storing in the pantry, asking yourself the same two questions: Is the date still good? Do I really want this for my new healthy lifestyle? Stay focused on making clear, fast decisions and don't look back. It will feel SO good to walk into your kitchen and know you have easy access to healthy fuel!

Bonus Tip: We'll talk more about cleaning and organizing in Chapter 7, but for now, before you put that food back in your refrigerator or pantry, make this easy spray to wipe everything down. It's non-toxic, effective, and inexpensive! Use it to clean surfaces throughout your home.

ALL-PURPOSE CLEANING SPRAY

Ingredients

30 Lemon, Lavender, Peppermint or Wild Orange Essential Oil (or a combination of these oils)

1/4 cup white vinegar

1 3/4 cups water

16 oz spray bottle

Method

Add all the ingredients to the spray bottle, shake and spray to clean surfaces.

ESSENTIAL TAKE CARE TIP

#32 Easy Healthy Swaps

When it comes to making healthy changes in your diet, be gentle with yourself. Too much, too fast, and you'll be overwhelmed. Make it easy with little modifications to what you're already eating. To eat more whole grains for example, use brown rice instead of white when you make stuffed peppers. Use whole wheat macaroni in your mac and cheese. Use whole grain bread crumbs in your meatloaf mix.

Ground turkey instead of ground beef for burgers and chili is another smart substitution. Top salads with flavored vinegar (Balsamic or Rice vinegar for example), and a splash of olive oil. For the salad itself, the more color the better! Choose a variety of dark, leafy greens, instead of iceberg. Healthier alternatives are often found right beside the things you may be putting in your shopping cart now. Take just a few minutes to look at the other options.

It's easy to substitute store-bought salad dressings with something you can make yourself:

ALL-PURPOSE CITRUS VINAIGRETTE

Ingredients

2 Lemon or Wild Orange Essential Oil

2 tablespoons apple cider vinegar

1 teaspoon honey

1/4 teaspoon salt

1/2 teaspoon ground mustard

1 tablespoon grated onion

4 tablespoons extra virgin olive oil

Method

Whisk together in a small bowl.

ESSENTIAL TAKE CARE TIP

#33 Go Fresh

Cook with seasonal, fresh foods whenever possible. In-season foods are less expensive, and many times faster to prepare. They are also bursting with flavor so you don't need to spend a lot of time with seasonings. And speaking of seasonings, using fresh ingredients will help to keep your sodium intake in check.

For a fast vegetable dish, cut vegetables into chunks, marinate in some homemade dressing, and then grill or broil 'til done to your liking. You can play around with flavors in this dressing. With 2 tablespoons apple cider vinegar and 4 tablespoons Olive Oil as your base, add just a drop of Basil, Oregano, Rosemary, or Thyme.

ESSENTIAL TAKE CARE TIP

#34 Glaze it Up

We've talked about why eating your vegetables is important...here's another way you can "dress them up" so you don't get bored. This recipe comes to us from a woman you already love from Chapter 1 (she brought us the Raspberry and Wild Orange Ganache Truffle recipe). Tenina Holder is a best-selling cookbook author and recipe developer in Australia. She's spent over a decade teaching people how to "dominate their kitchen" with her variety of cookbooks and masterclasses that sell out in minutes. She's passionate about helping people cook and enjoy real food at home with their families.

HONEY MUSTARD BUTTER GLAZE

Ingredients	Method
10 Black Pepper Essential Oil 5 Lemon Essential Oil 2 tbsp Dijon mustard	Place all ingredients into a small saucepan and place onto a medium heat. Allow to melt and combine without boiling. Taste and adjust seasoning as desired. Whisk a little just to combine.
4 tbsp unsalted butter	Drizzle over steamed veggies of choice.
4 tbsp Honey Pinch Pink Salt Flakes to taste	You can pre make this and store it in a jar in the fridge then simply dollop a couple of spoonfuls onto the hot veggies as needed.

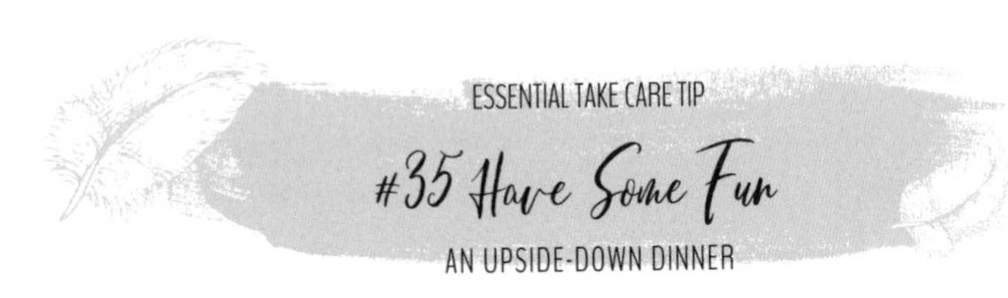

ESSENTIAL TAKE CARE TIP

#35 Have Some Fun

AN UPSIDE-DOWN DINNER

One of my kids' favorite dinners at our house is…breakfast! We love breakfast foods, but the mornings can be too rushed for everyone to enjoy a big, hot, sit-down meal. Turns out, breakfast foods are great any time of day.

For a speedy upside-down dinner, try pancakes or waffles. Add some fresh fruit and eggs or lean meat (turkey bacon for example) as a side dish, if you like, and you're all done. And here's where some of those substitutions will come in handy: instead of processed corn-syrup-based-syrup, use real maple syrup. A little goes a long way. Or you can heat up some frozen berries and mix them with honey.

Yogurt, granola, and fresh fruit make a great breakfast, or a dessert parfait at the end of the day. Anything will work as long as it's fresh and healthy.

Here's an easy recipe for granola you can make in your slow cooker! I don't remember where I saved this one from, but, it's fast, easy…and so good

SLOW COOKER GRANOLA

Ingredients

- 10 Lemon Essential Oil
- 1/2 cup honey
- 1/4 cup molasses
- 1/2 cup coconut or vegetable oil
- 4 cups quick cook oats
- 2 cups slivered almonds
- 1/2 cup chopped pecans
- 1 tsp unflavored protein powder (optional, but great for an extra boost!)
- 1 cup dried blueberries (you could also use dried cranberries)

Method

Turn crock pot on High and combine honey, molasses, oil, and Lemon Essential Oil, stir until melted together. In a medium size bowl, mix together the nuts, oats and protein powder (if you're using it). Pour that into the crock pot, and stir well to coat with the honey mixture. Cook for one and a half hours. Give it a stir every 30 minutes to prevent burning. Add in the dried blueberries or cranberries, and cook another 30 minutes. Spoon onto a tray (I line a baking sheet with parchment paper) and let cool. Store in an air tight container or bag for up to 10 days.

ESSENTIAL TAKE CARE TIP

#36 Mini Meals

Eat well, even on a busy day, by making the most of mini-meals. Some good examples of low-fuss ways to get your fuel include:

- Light cream cheese and spreadable fruit (or fresh fruit slices) on a bagel half or rice cake
- Apple slices with peanut butter or cheese chunks
- A mixed salad with beans and light dressing
- A cup of home-made soup (see Take Care Tip #40)
- Avocado Salad

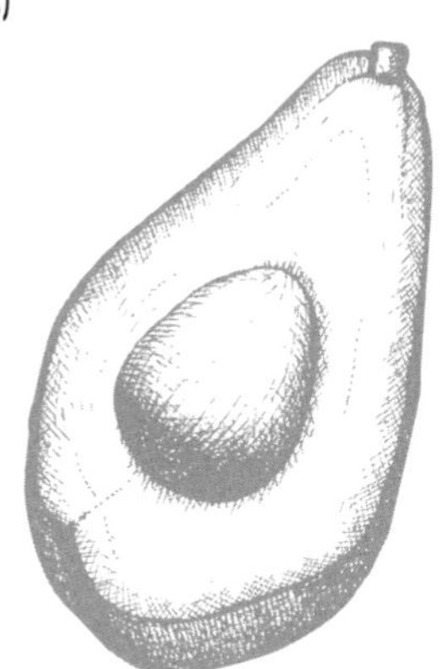

This easy recipe is packed with good things and easy to take with you for lunch or dinner on the go:

AVOCADO SALAD

Ingredients

2 Lime Essential Oil

1 Avocado

Handful of cherry or grape tomatoes

1 large or two small seedless cucumbers

1/4 to 1/2 red onion

3 Tbsp. Italian dressing

Method

Dice the avocado, cucumbers, and onion. Halve the tomatoes. Add all to a bowl and mix together. In a small bowl, whisk together the Italian dressing and the Lime Essential Oil. Pour over the salad, and mix to coat all ingredients.

ESSENTIAL TAKE CARE TIP

#37 Be Adventurous

HALOUMI AND WATERMELON SALAD

Ingredients

1lb red watermelon, sliced

2 Handful rocket or salad leaves of choice

Handful coriander leaves

Handful mint leaves

1 ripe avocado, diced

1/2 seedless cucumber, sliced

6oz Haloumi

DRESSING

Extra Virgin Olive Oil (EVOO) to taste

A drizzle of balsamic vinegar

5 Black Pepper Essential Oil

2 Turmeric Essential Oil

2 Cilantro Essential Oil

2 Lemon Essential Oil

Method

- Slice the watermelon, (I suggest bite sized pieces or wedges) Arrange on top of rocket in a serving bowl.
- Arrange the herbs over and all remaining ingredients except Haloumi.
- Cook the Haloumi in a medium hot frying pan with a little EVOO until golden and toasty on both sides.
- Add to the salad.
- Stir all the salad dressing ingredients together and drizzle over the salad just before serving.

ESSENTIAL TAKE CARE TIP

#38 Fruit Salad With Honey Lime Dressing

Did you know how much goodness is packed into the fruit you eat? Besides being an excellent source of vitamins and minerals, studies show people who eat fruit have a reduced risk of a variety of chronic diseases. Nutritionists recommend making half your plate fruits and vegetable for healthy meals. The nutrients found in fruit are powerful tools to help your body. The potassium in fruit has been shown to reduce the risk of heart attack and stroke, and may also lower your chances of getting kidney stones and bone density loss as you age.

Folate (folic acid) helps the body make red blood cells. If you are pregnant, or want to be, your doctor will talk with you about the need for folate during your first trimester. It helps prevent neural tube birth defects, like spina bifida.

1 to 2-1/2 cups of fruit are recommended each day, depending on how many calories you need. Fruit salads are a great ways to get all of that good stuff into your belly!

HONEY LIME FRUIT SALAD

Ingredients

Cut up melons, apples, pears, pineapple, and/or bananas. Use berries, grapes, or whatever's in season.

Method

Serve with a light honey dressing made with 2-3 Tablespoons honey and 2 drops of Lime Essential Oil. Mix that together in a little bowl, then pour over the fruit and stir.

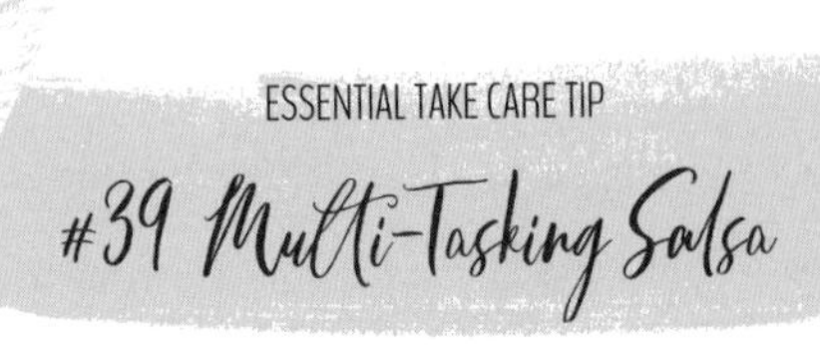

ESSENTIAL TAKE CARE TIP

#39 Multi-Tasking Salsa

Salsa is so good, so good for you, and so easy to make fresh in your kitchen. Once you do it yourself, you probably won't go back to buying it in a jar. The other great thing about salsa; you can use it for more than tortilla chips. I'll show you.

JEN'S FAVORITE HOMEMADE SALSA

Ingredients

1 large tomato

1 or 2 cloves of fresh garlic (I use one, but some of my garlic-loving friends use two)

1/2 of a large sweet onion

1 small bunch of fresh cilantro (I've always had good luck growing my own-you can also dip a toothpick into Cilantro Essential Oil and swirl that in your salsa.)

A few squeezes of fresh lemon juice (or one drop of Lemon Essential Oil)

Method

I use a hand chopper and chop the garlic first. Then I add the onion and chop, and then the tomato and chop. I finish by adding the cilantro and the fresh lemon juice, and then I chop a little more. If you like, you can add a pinch of salt and pepper, too.

You can serve it with baked tortilla chips and cut up veggies. A word of warning: Make it right before you want to eat it. The longer it sits, the more the garlic flavoring comes out. If you know you will be storing it in the fridge for a while, definitely go with just one clove of garlic.

Your job now is to decide where to use this multi-tasking salsa:

- Top toasted french baguette slices that have been brushed with olive oil (kind of a Mexican bruschetta)

- Use cold or hot as a sauce for pasta. Garnish with some reduced or low-fat cheddar cheese.
- Use as a topping for grilled chicken, fish, or your favorite egg dish.
- Use as a base for a pita sandwich. Add shredded low-fat cheddar cheese, some lettuce, and a little bit of reduced-fat sour cream.

ESSENTIAL TAKE CARE TIP

#40 Soup's On

What is it about soup? A Frenchman known as the king of chefs had a great way of putting it:

"Soup puts the heart at ease, calms down the violence of hunger, eliminates the tension of the day, and awakens and refines the appetite." — Auguste Escoffier

For our modern world, soup soothes. It's also a smart way to have healthy food ready when you are. It freezes well too, so make it in bulk, ladle it into individual-sized plastic containers and reheat them whenever you want a good snack or quick, light lunch.

Chef Pasquale Vericella say, "Make your own chicken broth, or buy it in quarts and keep it as a staple in your refrigerator. Quickly put together a healthy chicken soup by adding your favorite vegetables. I like a head of escarole, celery, carrots, tomatoes, and fresh parsley. Don't forget sea salt and cracked pepper."

You can use a drop of Black Pepper Essential Oil in this Recipe, and also experiment with using Thyme, Lemon, and Lemongrass Essential Oils to change the flavor.

ESSENTIAL TAKE CARE TIP

#41 Herb Pairings

Fresh herbs can help you quickly and easily flavor your food (and give even store-bought dishes a fresh homemade taste). Many herbs will help to fill your kitchen with relaxing aromas, too. However, using herbs in our cooking can bring so many more benefits! And, when fresh isn't readily available, quality Essential Oils are wonderful to have on hand---they have a longer shelf-life, and they're potent, so you'll use less, making them very cost-effective.

Chopped basil is fantastic in pasta dishes and salads.	Cilantro is great in rice, bean or vegetable dishes.	Oregano is good in salads of all kinds.
Dill is wonderful in salad dressing or as a garnish for fish.	Rosemary can be added to grilled chicken, fish, or potatoes.	Cinnamon for oatmeal, with apples, and in other baked goods.

Here are examples of powerful health benefits we get from a few common natural seasonings:

Black Pepper - a potent antioxidant that also has antibacterial and anti-inflammatory properties. Black pepper has also been shown to cause your stomach to increase the production of hydrochloric acid, which helps with digestion. Some research suggest black pepper can support your nervous system and metabolism!

Ginger –With anti-inflammatory properties, Ginger may help to soothe sore muscles, menstrual cramps, and headaches. It also soothes your intestinal tract, promotes healthy digestion, and works to calm nausea. Ginger has also been shown to curb cravings.

Turmeric - One of the active ingredients is curcumin, which is a powerful antioxidant and anti-inflammatory. New benefits of curcumins are being researched including immune system support, and improved joint function.

ESSENTIAL TAKE CARE TIP

#42 Bone Broth

This tip is another one from the "everything old is new again" files! Your Grandma probably made broth for soup this way. We often think of soup as a comfort food...a go-to when we need to warm and soothe the soul. Bone both is a trend in the fitness, holistic, and foodie circles, and many people are singing its praises!

This recipe was contributed by Jackie Ritz, author and creator of www.thepaleomama.com. Jackie is a farmer, herbalist, gardener and lover of real, unprocessed food. Her passions for food and natural healing have become the foundation for both her published books, Everyday Natural and The Home Apothecary.

According to an old South American proverb, "good broth will resurrect the dead." While that's undoubtedly an exaggeration, it speaks to the value placed on this wholesome food, going back through the annals of time.

Jackie says first and foremost, homemade bone broth is excellent for speeding healing and recuperation from illness. You've undoubtedly heard the old adage that chicken soup will help cure a cold, and there's scientific support for such a statement. However, there are so many more benefits of homemade bone broth.

HOMEMADE BONE BROTH BENEFITS

- Helps heal and seal your gut, and promotes healthy digestion
- Inhibits infection
- Reduces joint pain and inflammation
- Fights inflammation
- Promotes healthy hair and nail growth
- Promotes strong and healthy bones

The healing power of bone broth comes when it is gelatin-rich. Using bones from pastured or wild ruminants and poultry will give you the most nutritious bone broth.

If you are new to making bone broth, then Jackie recommends you start with chicken bones, since it is the most palatable for beginners.

HOW TO USE BONE BROTH

Bone broth is essential to soups, stews, and even many sauteed dishes. If you come to enjoy the taste of it, you might even enjoy a hot mug of bone broth on a cold day. Jackie says she loves to add a slice of lemon to her mug of broth and a sprinkle of sea salt.

Bone broth freezes very well too. You can freeze small batches in ice cube trays or in a ziploc bag (lay it flat to save space).

SLOW BONE BROTH

Ingredients

2 pounds of high quality bones (beef, bison, chicken, lamb, or pork)

1/2 cup of apple cider vinegar

2 carrots, chopped

2 celery stalks, chopped

4 garlic cloves

2 bay leaves

1 large onion, peeled and chopped

2 teaspoons of dried thyme, or less than 1 drop Thyme Essential Oil

1/2 cup of dried mushrooms or 1 cup of fresh

1 tablespoon of black peppercorns

Filtered water

Method

- For beef or bison bones, Jackie recommends roasting the beef bones to help increase flavor. To do this, simply place the beef bones on a sheet pan and roast in the oven until well browned at 375F. Drain the fat, then transfer the bones to your slow cooker. Skip this step if using chicken bones.
- Add all the ingredients to your crockpot, except water. Fill to the top with filtered water.
- Turn on high for one hour, then reducing to low for 5–24 hours. The longer you cook your bone broth, the more nutritious it becomes.
- If water evaporates, add a little more to keep the stock filled.
- Cool the stock and then strain through a colander covered with a cheesecloth or old t-shirt.
- Use within 4 days or freeze.
- If you do not own a slow cooker, you can make bone broth on your stovetop. Simply follow all the directions above, but do not add more than 1 gallon of water.

ESSENTIAL TAKE CARE TIP

#43 Go Bright!

Let yourself gravitate toward bright colors when you're shopping for produce. Brighter, deeper-colored fruits and vegetables don't just look prettier, they also have greater concentrations of important antioxidants, vitamins and minerals. The more color you can put on your plate, the better. It's a no-brainer way to dramatically increase your intake of important vitamins and minerals.

Fruit and veggies straight from the store (or farm) are covered in bacteria and other contaminants. Some fruits are even coated with a layer of wax to make them last longer in the stores. We can use Essential Oils to wash our produce in a non-toxic way. Get into a habit of washing what you bring home before you even put it in the fridge.

Just put whatever fruits and vegetables you'd like to wash in the sink and fill the sink with water 'til it covers the produce. Add 1 cup of vinegar and 5 drops of Lemon Essential Oil. Let soak for 15-20 minutes, scrub and rinse clean.

You can also make a spray by just adding 7-10 drops of Lemon Essential Oil to a 4oz spray bottle. Fill to the top with water. Shake and spray on fruits and vegetables and wipe clean as needed.

ESSENTIAL TAKE CARE TIP

#44 Stress-Busting Smoothie

Here's an easy-to-make treat that will also help to calm your nerves:

- Blend some low-fat milk or almond milk, ice, a banana, and 2 drops of Wild Orange Essential Oil together and enjoy.
- The banana and the milk boost the brain chemicals dopamine and serotonin, which help to regulate and reduce stress and anxiety.
- The Wild Orange will give you a happy mood boost. If you find that you need a little extra boost during the day, try adding some unsweetened protein powder to your shake for a snack or a mini-meal.

Any amount of time you take for yourself is important. Taking yourself out of "caregiver mode" for as little as ten minutes in the middle of a full day helps you connect with who you are in a larger sense. Ten minute breaks add up, and play an important role in preventing you from becoming consumed by other obligations and responsibilities.

CHAPTER FIVE

Go to Bed

Do you remember what healthy sleep is? You might see people in movies doing it. They generally lie down in a comfortable bed, close their eyes, and stay that way for a nice, long while. It looks so peaceful. Why can't we do that? In this chapter, we'll focus on how you can start getting the quality sleep you need.

Statistics (unfortunately) show that it would probably be a great idea to start an overnight Essential Take Care Tips Club. The National Sleep Foundation reports that a lot of people are awake then! In fact, more than half of the adults in the United States say they experience sleep problems more than once a week. Two-thirds of the elderly people interviewed for the survey said they have frequent sleep problems. In fact, about 40,000,000 people in the US alone have diagnosed sleep disorders – and -- fewer than three percent of those people are being treated for it!

How did something so natural turn into such an issue?

WHAT'S THE BIG DEAL?

Well for those who don't have any trouble getting to sleep, it's hard to understand what could be the problem. But, for those who struggle just to let their bodies and brains enjoy a little rest, it's a huge deal! Often, the more that we think about not being able to sleep, the more stressed we get, and the more we can't sleep. It's a bad cycle.

Plain and simple, humans need sleep. Sleep is essential to our health and well-being. It helps our brains recharge and recover from stress, and it repairs the cellular damage our bodies experience every single day. Most experts agree that somewhere between seven and nine hours of sleep is ideal for most of us. When we get fewer than six hours of sleep, we start to notice serious side effects related to our mood, our ability to function, and our body's ability to fend off disease.

This is something we all need to pay more attention to because lack of sleep can shorten our life span. Perhaps you remember hearing about a British study on lack of sleep released in 2007. For 17 years, researchers tracked sleep patterns and the health status of 10,000 government workers. The study found that people who regularly get five hours of sleep or less double their risk of dying of heart disease, and, due to their weakened, sleep-deprived state, are at significantly higher risk of dying at a younger age from other diseases as well! In other studies, lack of sleep has been linked to an increased risk of diabetes, heart disease, obesity, and cancers.

When we don't get enough sleep, we are at greater risk of other kinds of dangers, too. The National Highway Traffic Safety Administration reports that drowsy or sleeping drivers cause at least 100,000 auto accidents every year (a conservative number, since it only reflects the reported incidents).

It's not surprising that chances of work-related accidents, mistakes, and injuries go way up when employees haven't had enough sleep. In fact, some of the more tragic, history-making examples of on-the-job accidents have been traced to sleep-deprived night shift workers: the space shuttle Challenger disaster, the Three Mile Island nuclear accident, and the Alaskan Exxon Valdez oil spill, to name just a few.

But even if the physical health implications weren't so grave, we know from experience that when we don't get enough sleep it affects everything we do throughout the day. It's harder to learn new things quickly, we can't do our jobs as well, our stamina goes down, we lose energy and our memory gets fuzzy. When we're tired, we're grouchy, mean, irritable, and even angry. How can we possibly provide critical, loving care for ourselves, or anyone else when we're feeling like that?

If you're a caregiver, you may be managing and administering medications. You are responsible for your own health and safety, as well as the health and safety of the person you're caring for. This is a lot of important work to entrust to someone who's overtired. When we aren't able to get enough recovery time for our bodies and brains, we're setting ourselves up for the possibility of much more than a few yawns the next day.

Now, you may be thinking, "Oh I'm doing just fine on [fill in with some number less than seven] hours of sleep a night. I'm just wired like that!" but listen to this: Dr. Daniel Shade, director of the Allegheny General Hospital Sleep Disorder Center, told me that our brains are able to adapt to lack of sleep, to the point that the effects of chronic sleep deprivation start to feel normal!

So that makes it even more important to remember that even if you're feeling functional and fine, your body is just absolutely not able to function the way it should if you don't give yourself enough recovery between your demanding days. "When people are sleep-deprived, their performance level decreases," Dr. Shade says. "But there's a disconnect between how you think you're doing and how you're actually doing."

"It's sneaky," he added. "Like carbon monoxide poisoning."

What happens during sleep?

To look at a person sleeping, it doesn't seem like much at all is going on – but major repair work is happening. First of all, a growth hormone is released. That's why sleep is so important for children. But adults need that hormone too. It helps rebuild muscle tissue. The brain is also very busy while we're snoozing. It sends signals that allow us to pass through the different important phases, or levels of sleep:

We start with a light sleep, during which we can easily be awakened. As we continue to drift off, our brain activity slows down. We spend about half of our total sleep time in this floaty phase.

Next comes a deeper sleep, in which your body temperature drops and your muscles relax. This is when the immune system repairs any damage the body sustained during the day. In sleep studies, researchers use devices that pick up very slow brain waves – called Delta waves – during this time. There's no dreaming. Our minds are allowed to drift and let go of daily pressures. Our unconscious mind becomes more in control. Think of this as a deep, trance-like period of intense relaxation. This phase, by the way, is where infants spend most of their sleep time.

We actually go through two back to back phases of deep sleep, but suffice it to say, we're totally conked out for a while. If you woke up from these phases, you'd be pretty groggy.

After this comes the much-studied Rapid Eye-Movement sleep, or REM sleep. In this phase, our breathing becomes faster and shallower. Our eyes dart around quickly behind our eyelids. Our arms and legs experience temporary paralysis and our heart rate and blood pressure go up.

I didn't get this stuff from a horror flick; this is really what happens, and it's all very natural, normal, and needed. REM sleep is when most of our emotional and mental restoration happens, and when we dream the most. Regarding dreams: Sleep researchers and some psychologists believe that these flights of imagination actually allow us to sort and clear out our thoughts and then retain and organize the most important information we learned during our day.

It takes 90-120 minutes to go through all of these phases – and this is what is called the sleep cycle. To operate at our optimum level, we must go through the sleep cycle several times throughout the night.

With all this work to be done while we're sleeping, it's clear that if we don't get enough sleep, our brains and bodies will run, but definitely not at peak performance.

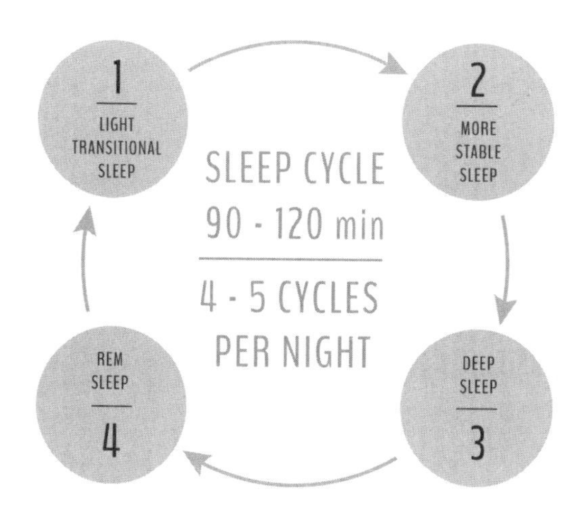

WHAT'S KEEPING US UP AT NIGHT?

Worry? Stress? Pain? A little bit of everything? Why, if it's so important, do we struggle to get to sleep…or stay that way?

As caregivers, we feel like we need to be "on" all the time. We have SO much to do, and it never feels like we have enough time to do it, so we get into the habit of staying up later to do just a few…more…things.

The next thing you know, it's 2:30 in the morning, and you have to be up for work at six. You collapse into bed, physically exhausted, but your brain won't stop (blasted brain!). You start to think about everything you have to do in the morning. What didn't you get done today? How are you going to fit it all in tomorrow? Great, now it's a little after 3, and you've got less than three hours to bring your body back to a refreshed, renewed state. That's just not enough time for sleep to work its magic.

When you consider the extra stress that caregiving brings, it's normal that we would have an occasional rough night. Our bodies were designed to handle this from time to time. But if you start to find that it's difficult to fall asleep or stay asleep most nights, it's important to be evaluated for insomnia. There is nothing wrong in calling for help if you need it in this area, in fact, insomnia and other sleep disorders are more common than you might think.

More women than men are diagnosed with insomnia, and older people are more prone to it than younger people. Major, prolonged stress can cause insomnia. Anything that changes or disrupts your sleep schedule (travel, or a different shift at work, for example) can cause it too. Your sleep troubles can continue even after the original cause goes away, because, like we talked about earlier, your brain can seem to adapt to a lack of sleep, and fool you into thinking you're doing just fine. It's easy for unhealthy sleep patterns to become a learned, accepted routine. Don't be fooled!

Insomnia can be chronic, or short-term, and can be related to a variety of things:

Anxiety – deep, frequent feelings of worry, fear, helplessness, and hopelessness.

Stress – the pressure of coping with all the things in your life that require some kind of response from you.

Depression – an all-too-common mental disorder that can make you feel very sad, tired, and discouraged.

Hormonal changes – whether it's PMS, pregnancy, or menopause, or everything in between, our hormones fluctuate constantly, and may affect our sleep.

Age – as we get older, our melatonin levels decrease. Melatonin is a hormone that helps to promote and control sleep.

Pain – muscle strains, stiff necks, and sore backs and joints are common sleep thieves.

Your Genes – some studies show that sleep problems may be linked to family history.

Medications – many prescription and over-the-counter drugs can cause insomnia. Ask your doctor or pharmacist about the possible side effects of your medication. Speak up about any sleep problems you may be having. Sometimes, it may simply be an issue of taking your medications at a different time of day...but talk to your doctor first before you make any changes to your medical treatment.

DON'T FIGHT NATURE!

All of the major systems in our bodies depend on rest and sleep to rebuild for the next day and start fresh. Before the invention of electricity, people went to bed when the sun went down and woke up when it came back up. Businesses also closed much earlier in the day. There was no overnight shift. We live much differently now. Changes in our culture have forced our bodies to change, and in some cases, to work against our powerful natural instincts.

When you think about it like that, it's easy to understand why your body reacts the way it does when you don't go to bed when you're tired, or allow yourself to wake up naturally when your body says it's time. You're interfering with your body's natural instincts, and your body's fighting back!

SO WHAT CAN WE DO?

The good news in all of this is that doctors who deal with sleep disorders are having great success with sleep treatments and therapies. Dr. Shade says that after just a few weeks of getting more consistent, quality sleep, patients say they feel like a new person. They are happier, more energetic, ambitious, and satisfied with what they are able to accomplish.

That's where I want you to be. So, right off that bat, I want you to make sure that you're getting proper treatment for any underlying illnesses (cardiovascular disease and diabetes, for example) that can interfere with sleep. I also want you to tell your doctor or pharmacist about any over-the-counter or home-remedy types of medications you might be using to help you fall asleep. A number of pharmacies are equipped with a system that will automatically check any medication you take against your other prescriptions, to make sure they're compatible.

Next, try keeping a sleep diary. It can be a notebook that you keep by your bed. In the morning, date the top of the page, and then note the things leading up to or perhaps connected to the sleep you just had. Examples of what you might write in your sleep diary are: what you ate or drank before you went to bed, any specific stress-causing incident that happened, if you exercised that day, when you went to bed and when you woke up, how long it took you to fall asleep, how restful the sleep seemed, and if you woke up during the night. This will help both you and your doctor identify any trends, make a diagnosis, and recommend a treatment if needed.

There. That gets you started, now let me tuck you in with my ten-minute tips for how to achieve a good night's sleep.

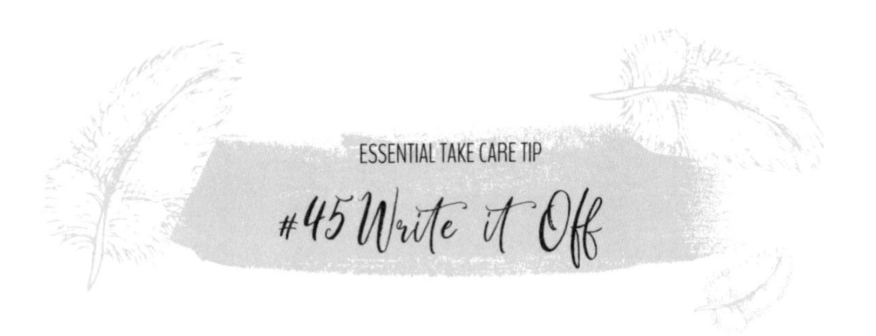

ESSENTIAL TAKE CARE TIP

#45 Write it Off

Are you having trouble falling asleep because your mind is like a huge to-do list? Get that stuff out of your brain. Keep a little note pad and pen on your nightstand so that you can quickly and easily jot those thoughts down when they pop into your head. It's simple, but it works. By writing the thought down, you can rest easier with a clear, relaxed mind, knowing you won't forget about it in the morning. Psychology teaches us there's big benefit in the act of actually writing it out, so even though this may seem like a little thing, don't underestimate its power!

Aromatherapy has been helping people with relaxation for centuries, and modern scientists are studying Essential Oils to get a better understanding of exactly how and why it can help with sleep. Preliminary research shows that breathing in Essential Oil molecules, or absorbing them through the skin, may trigger chemicals in the brain that control the quality of our sleep.

Here's an Essential Oil diffuser blend you can use to help you to drift into the night:

QUIET THE BRAIN

Ingredients	
2	Vetiver Essential Oil
2	Frankincense Essential Oil
2	Bergamot Essential Oil

Method

Following the instructions that came with your diffuser, add the Oils and water. Turn on the mist to experience the benefits.

Each of these Oils has complex chemical compounds that work to support a healthy brain and emotions in a variety of ways. This blend will help soothe your mind so you can relax and go to sleep.

ESSENTIAL TAKE CARE TIP

#46 Talk Yourself Down

Are you too frustrated or angry, to sleep? If you're mad because you're being stretched too thin, or because a loved one is sick, staying angry will make it very difficult to get a good night's sleep. Here's a deceptively easy positive-thinking technique that psychologists have used for years: **BELIEVE** that you **WILL FEEL** however you tell yourself to feel. I know, this one sounds too easy, but you'll be surprised by your own power to talk yourself down.

Start by remembering that you don't have to lose the anger, you just have to put it to bed for a while so you can rest too. For example, if you're angry, think to yourself, "I am really mad that I'm the only one running around taking care of Dad and that no one appreciates how much I do." That's the anger part. Now here's where you take instant control of it. Think to yourself, "But I am choosing right now to feel calm, relaxed, and secure." As you repeat this phrase over and over, try to breathe slowly and deeply.

Soon, you should feel calmer, more relaxed, and more secure. The anger will still be there if you want to get back to it – you're not throwing it away – but this thought process gives you the power of control. With it, you'll feel like you're the one in charge of that emotion, not the other way around, and that feeling of power and security will help you to relax and fall asleep.

Doctors who use this kind of technique with their patients say that it helps to balance the body's energy and gives fast and long-lasting relief for insomnia.

Aromatherapy is wonderful to help with powerful emotions of anger, and grief. Like we talked about in the Introduction, just breathing in a scent can trigger a release of chemicals from the brain that will help with coping and calming.

Make a Calming Spray that you can spray on yourself, your sheets or pillow at night; and then take with you to use during your day, as well.

CALMING SPRAY

Ingredients

3 **Lime** Essential Oil
cleanses negativity,
brings happy energy

2 **Lavender** Essential Oil
helps you to slow down

2 **Frankincense** Essential Oil
supports rational thinking

1 **Peppermint** Essential Oil
energy to lift you up from any negativity

1 **Clove Bud** Essential Oil
stimulates warm, settled feelings,
helps you to move forward

Witch Hazel (optional)

4 oz glass spray bottle

Method

Add the Oils to the spray bottle. Fill to the top with Witch Hazel. Shake and spray to experience the benefits. Some people just use water to complete the spray, that's fine too, just make sure to shake before each use to help distribute the Oils.

Witch Hazel acts as a natural emulsifier, helping to keep the Oils distributed throughout the blend. On its own, Witch hazel is a powerhouse compound. It comes from the leaves and bark of a shrub native to North America. Throughout time, people have used it as a natural remedy for soothing a variety of skin irritations, and reducing inflammation. Today, Witch Hazel is commonly found in aftershaves, facial toners, insect bite sprays, hemorrhoid treatments, and more.

Visit www.TakeCareTips. for more Witch Hazel and Essential Oil spray recipes!

ESSENTIAL TAKE CARE TIP

#47 Take Control Of The Clock

Worrying about not being able to fall asleep only makes it even harder to fall asleep. Practice the old, "out of sight, out of mind" theory. Keep your alarm clock on the other side of the room and turn it so you can't see the numbers. Tossing and turning only to see 1:00…2:00…3:00…glowing in the darkness, will only make the situation worse.

Another way to keep the clock from ruling your night is to walk away. Sleep researchers say that if you can't fall asleep within about 20 minutes or so of hitting the pillow, get out of bed and do something else. Move to a chair to do some light reading, for example, or some journaling. Move back to bed when you're ready. The idea here is to break any habit you might have to associate your bed with the sleep struggle. Many sleep therapists tell people to turn the bedroom into a space for sleep and sex-period. No reading or watching TV in bed. No catching up on work there, either.

When you're feeling restless, your sweet self needs peace. There are beautiful pre-made Essential Oil blends that support peaceful feelings: a Restful blend, a Grounding blend, a Reassuring blend, a Comforting blend.

You can also make your own using some of the Oils featured in those blends:

SETTLE DOWN DIFFUSER BLEND

Ingredients

2 **Lavender** Essential Oil

2 **Hawaiian Sandalwood** Essential Oil

1 **Vetiver** Essential Oil

1 **Ylang Ylang** Essential Oil

10 ml Rollerball Bottle (optional)

Method

Following the manufacturers instructions, add Oils to your diffuser.

For a rollerball blend add 5 drops of Lavender and Hawaiian Sandalwood along with a drop pf Vetiver and Ylang Ylang to a 10ml bottle and fill the rest of the way with Fractionated Coconut Oil. Roll on the bottoms of your feet, inside of elbows or wrists, or the back of the neck.

ESSENTIAL TAKE CARE TIP

#48 Have A Little Something

Remember grandma's warm milk sleep remedy? Well, there's some science behind it. All dairy foods are a good source of an amino acid called tryptophan. Our body converts tryptophan to the hormones melatonin and serotonin, which in turn have been linked to achieving quality sleep. (Other sources of tryptophan are oats, peanuts, bananas, and poultry). If you want to try a bedtime snack that will help you nod off more easily (rather than a glass of warm milk) eat a carbohydrate with a little bit of protein. This mix appears to be the best for increasing tryptophan levels in the brain.

So, you could have a small bowl of oatmeal or cereal with milk, a few crackers with peanut butter, or an apple and a piece of cheese, for example.

Now, just when I have you hungry, I need to point out that eating too much before you go to bed, especially too much protein, will work against you. Food with a lot of protein also contains an amino acid called tyrosine that works to stimulate brain activity, which you don't want when you're trying to wind down. So, skip the leftover chicken wings! Also, late-night eating is, of course, not the best way to control your weight. A 2017 study published in the American Journal of Clinical Nutrition found that those who eat before bed have higher amounts of body fat.

The snack ideas I offered will fill you up, help to bring on restful sleep, and even help you wake up with more energy, without working against your weight management efforts.

Here's one more:

Fruit & Yogurt Bedtime Snack

To a half cup of your favorite plain, no-sugar added yogurt, stir in one drop Lime Essential Oil. Mix in a handful of fresh berries (I like raspberries and blueberries for this). If you don't have fresh berries, thawed frozen berries will work, too...just make sure you're buying no-sugar added varieties.

ESSENTIAL TAKE CARE TIP

#49 Feel The Rhythm Of The Night

Ever wonder why we turn off the lights to go to sleep? I mean have you ever thought about why we feel awake when it's bright and sunny, and sleepy when the only light we see comes from the moon and stars? It's because the cycle of light and dark, sunrise and sunset, all fit perfectly with a function in our bodies called the circadian rhythm. The circadian rhythm is governed by a pea-size master switch deep within our brains called the pineal gland. When the sun goes down, the darkness triggers our pineal gland to produce melatonin which makes us feel like curling up in a nice soft bed and staying there for a while. When the light starts shining again, the pineal gland stops producing melatonin, and sends new hormonal messages to our body that tell us to wake up and jump into a new day. We've got all of that programmed right in…how cool is that?!

This is the reason we get so wiped out when we switch to the night shift at work or when we travel and change time zones – we are going against our circadian rhythm.

Here's how we can get ourselves back into the rhythm of things: First of all, step outside and enjoy the sunlight a little bit every day. When our pineal gland knows it's daytime, it will also figure out that nighttime will come when it's supposed to. The next thing we can do is make sure that it's truly dark during the night. This will tell your pineal gland, "OK, now produce melatonin!" If streetlights are shining through your window, pull down the blinds; if your nightlights could double as spotlights, swap them out for something that glows rather than glares, or better yet if possible, get rid of them. Most importantly, turn off the TV while you're trying to get to sleep. The combination of light from the screen and noise will stimulate your brain no matter how tired you feel, and work against your body's own natural rhythm.

The concept of Anchoring can help us here. When we want to stay on track with a goal, for example, we can use a symbol or a word that helps us re-connect and re-focus just by glancing at the object or saying the word. We can anchor ourselves to night and day with an aromatherapy routine utilizing Essential Oils and some self-care.

Let's look at how you can get into habits that will help you acknowledge "day" and "night" and will set off a series of reactions in your brain that will help to keep you in rhythm.

AM/PM ANCHORING ROUTINES

AM: Rub a drop of Wild Orange Essential Oil between your palms upon waking, cup your hands over your nose and mouth, close your eyes, and take nice, slow breaths in and out. As you breathe in that bright, happy scent, you can add a positive morning affirmation; "I am grateful for the blessing of this beautiful, fresh new day, full of hope and opportunities."

PM: Rub a drop of Lavender Essential Oil between your palms as you're going to bed, cup your hands over your nose and mouth, close your eyes, and take nice, slow breaths in and out. As you breathe in the relaxing, comforting scent, you can add a positive bedtime affirmation; "I am grateful for all the good things I accomplished today. I release any tension, fear, or worry. I welcome the healing, joy, and energy I know will come from peaceful sleep."

Keep your Oils on your nightstand so you can take just a few minutes to do this every morning and night. Before long, you'll notice that just smelling Wild Orange will bring about those positive feelings…same with Lavender.

ESSENTIAL TAKE CARE TIP

#50 Exercise For Sleep

Sorry, but I have to say it again: exercise! Many studies show that regular exercise, especially cardio exercise – really, anything that gets your heart pumping – will help you achieve healthy, quality sleep.

It seems to encourage your body to move more easily between those sleep phases I told you about earlier. And when your body experiences focused, stimulating activity during the day, it will demand deeper, restorative sleep at night.

So, to improve the quality of your sleep, aim to raise that heart rate for 30 minutes a day, five to six times a week. As you know already, this will make a difference in quite a few areas of your life. Remember, too, that three 10-minute chunks of activity are just as effective as one 30 minute lump. Those smaller exercise breaks will probably be a little easier for you to fit into your day.

A word of caution: Timing is everything. If you exercise too close to bedtime your body might get too revved up to go to sleep easily. To give your body ample time to ease into the evening, try to fit your activity in before dinner, or take a walk soon afterwards.

A nice post exercise massage will go a long way to helping you wind down as well. You can buy pre-made Essential Oil Soothing Blends, or you can make your own, like this natural salve that will soothe your muscles and joints so you can relax. Clove and Black Pepper Essential Oils will provide warmth, while Peppermint and Eucalyptus are cooling. All of these Oils are known to help reduce inflammation, as well.

SOOTHING SALVE

Ingredients

40	Clove Essential Oil
20	Black Pepper Essential Oil
20	Peppermint Essential Oil
40	Eucalyptus Essential Oil

1/4 cup virgin coconut oil (this is the solid coconut oil)

3 tablespoons extra virgin olive oil

4 oz Mason jar

small saucepan

water

2 tablespoons beeswax pellets
(sold at craft stores, and at various places online)

wooden craft stick (optional)

Method

Add coconut oil, olive oil, and beeswax pellets to your Mason jar (it'll fit, but will be full!)

Place the filled Mason jar into the saucepan. Add enough water so that it covers about 3/4 of the jar.

Warm the mixture over medium-low heat 'til melted and smooth. Carefully stir the mixture during this process. You may want to use a wooden craft stick for this, to simplify clean up.

The jar will be hot, use oven mitts to take it out of the saucepan and place it on a hot pad or surface that can handle the heat. Next, add 40 drops each of the Clove and Eucalyptus Oils, and 20 drops each of the Peppermint and Black Pepper Essential Oils. Stir well to combine.

Let cool (can take up to 12 hours to fully set).

You can scoop a little out and warm it between your palms, then massage into the neck, shoulders, joints, and don't forget the feet! Make sure to wash your hands after you use it to avoid getting any in your eyes.

ESSENTIAL TAKE CARE TIP

#51 Get With The Program

If you're a parent, you probably know about how important it is for children to have a consistent routine when it comes to bedtime. Well, it's just as good for adults.

Create a little bedtime routine for yourself. Even ten minutes of quiet time and deep breathing, brushing your hair, massaging your hands and feet, or some light, careful stretching is enough to make you feel comforted and relaxed. Turn down the lights, anything to slow the mind, and let the day go. Whatever your special routine, it will become a signal to your body that it's time to change modes.

A bath is also a great way to unwind. In fact, in ancient times, people took daily aromatic baths, which they believed would prolong their lives!

Adding Essential Oils to your bath is a quick and easy way to create an at-home spa experience that will help you melt away the stress of the day, and set the tone for a relaxing night.

BEDTIME SOAK

Ingredients

- 6 Roman Chamomile Essential Oil
- 4 Wild Orange Essential Oil
- 2 Sandalwood Essential Oil
- 1/ 3 cup sea salt
- 1/3 cup Epsom salt
- 1/4 cup baking soda
- Mason Jar

Method

Add all ingredients to a small bowl, mix together. Store in a Mason jar. Add 1/4 to 1/2 cup to a warm bath and soak for ten minutes.

ESSENTIAL TAKE CARE TIP

#52 The Goodnight Wiggle

This one may sound a little silly, but…If you're having trouble falling asleep…try wiggling your toes! I learned this from an acupuncturist who was a guest on my TV talk show. Apparently, lying flat on your back and wiggling all of your toes up and down for a little while will help relax your whole body and soothe your brain.

Toe-wiggling is linked to the ancient science of Reflexology. This practice is based on the idea that everything in your body is connected, and that the different areas on your feet act like a kind of control panel for the rest of your body – your organs, your blood, your cells, your bones, your skin, and your brain. It's something many believe you can get very specific with…activating certain areas of the feet and toes for the purpose of supporting health and wellness to specific organs.

The action of wiggling your toes is thought to open up positive energy channels all through your body. With that kind of energy flowing easily through you, it's easier to rest and sleep.

While we're talking about toes, it's a good time for me to bring up the benefits of applying Essential Oils to the bottoms of your feet. The Oils are readily absorbed there, and traces are found throughout the body in less than 20 minutes. While our bodies are at rest, our systems are relaxed, and that's a great time to use Essential Oils and let them get to work while you sleep. Lavender and Frankincense are two popular choices. You simply massage a drop of either into the bottom of each foot. Experiment with other Oils and Blends that can help to support you as needed…a Protective Blend for immune support, or a Respiratory Support Blend, for example.

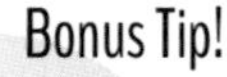

Bonus Tip!

Wiggling your toes first thing in the morning before you get out of bed is said to jump-start that flow of energy and make you feel ready for your day. Seriously!

Here's a very basic reflex point chart that may assist you with the application of Essential Oils in the regions of the foot.

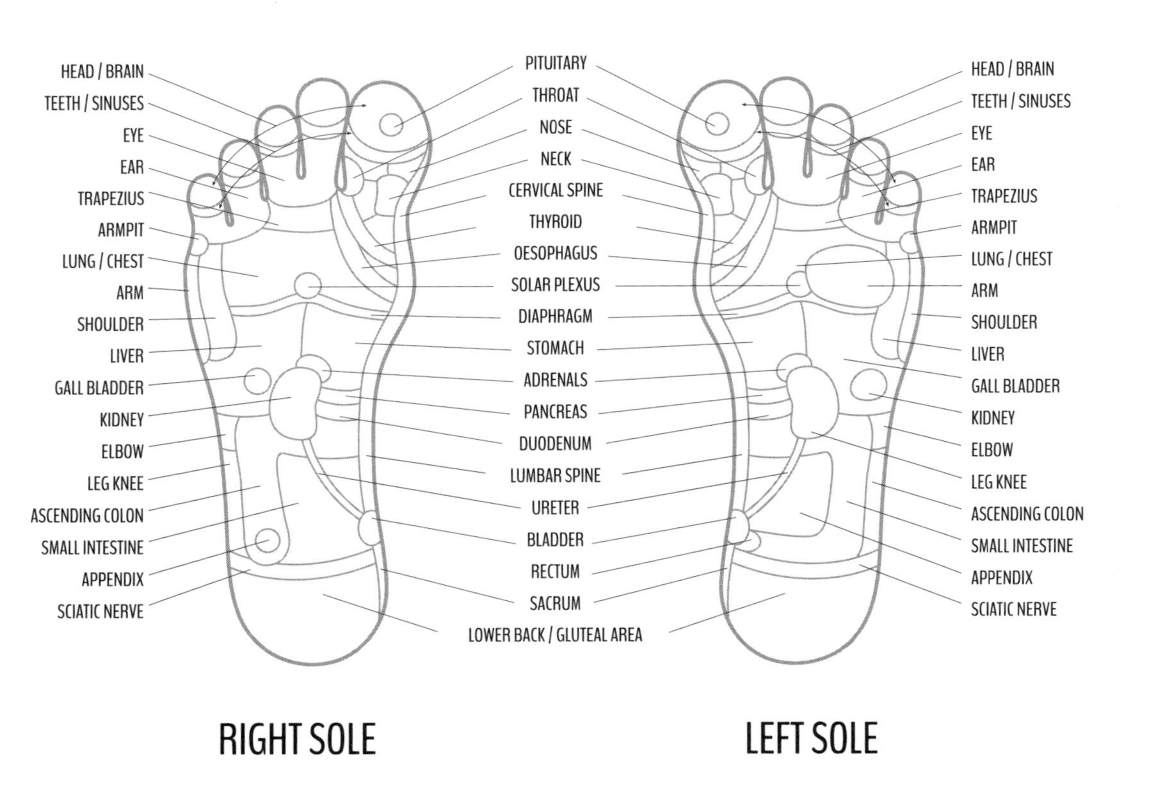
HEAD / BRAIN
TEETH / SINUSES
EYE
EAR
TRAPEZIUS
ARMPIT
LUNG / CHEST
ARM
SHOULDER
LIVER
GALL BLADDER
KIDNEY
ELBOW
LEG KNEE
ASCENDING COLON
SMALL INTESTINE
APPENDIX
SCIATIC NERVE
PITUITARY
THROAT
NOSE
NECK
CERVICAL SPINE
THYROID
OESOPHAGUS
SOLAR PLEXUS
DIAPHRAGM
STOMACH
ADRENALS
PANCREAS
DUODENUM
LUMBAR SPINE
URETER
BLADDER
RECTUM
SACRUM
LOWER BACK / GLUTEAL AREA
HEAD / BRAIN
TEETH / SINUSES
EYE
EAR
TRAPEZIUS
ARMPIT
LUNG / CHEST
ARM
SHOULDER
LIVER
GALL BLADDER
KIDNEY
ELBOW
LEG KNEE
ASCENDING COLON
SMALL INTESTINE
APPENDIX
SCIATIC NERVE
RIGHT SOLE
LEFT SOLE

ESSENTIAL TAKE CARE TIP

#53 Ditch The Drinking

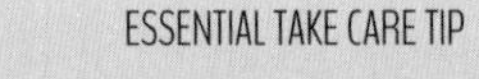

I'm not going to charge you a minute for this tip; in fact, I'm going to save you time. I want you to stop fixing drinks that contain caffeine or alcohol before bedtime. Of course it's good not to drink too much of anything close to bedtime, because you know what that will do in a few hours.

Alcohol and caffeine will interfere with your sleep in a different way. Some people say a glass of wine, beer, or a mixed drink helps them release tension and feel sleepy. That might be true – at first – but alcohol also interferes with your sleep cycle. A drink before bed makes your body struggle to drift into the deepest, most restorative sleep phases.

Caffeine, on the other hand, is a stimulant. It increases activity in your nervous system, which makes it harder to fall asleep. Lots of drinks, and even some over-the-counter pain medications contain high amounts of caffeine. Check the label and switch to something caffeine-free.

Both caffeine and alcohol contain chemical substances that make you crave them. Studies show that caregivers are more susceptible to harmful addictions due to searching for ways to escape daily stress. Could you be addicted? Recognizing something like that in yourself isn't always easy. A good place to start would be to try this tip: Can you go without alcohol or caffeine this week? If just that question makes you uncomfortable, maybe it's time to talk with someone and get some help.

Essential Oils are being used along with traditional therapies in helping people overcome addictions. They help to diminish cravings and support emotional health needed for recovery. Holistic practitioners I know recommend the following Oils to help with alcohol and caffeine addictions. A convenient way to keep them with you is to use them in nasal diffusers. Check out the Resource section at the end of this book, and www.TakeCareTips.com for ideas on where you can buy inhalers and other supplies.

ESSENTIAL OIL INHALER RECIPES

Ingredients	
FOR ALCOHOL ADDICTION	
1	Lavender Essential Oil
1	Lemongrass Essential Oil
1	Tea Tree Essential Oil
1	Rosemary Essential Oil
FOR CAFFEINE ADDICTION	
4	Bergamot Essential Oil

Method

To use Essential Oils with your nasal inhaler, just add the drops of Oil to the cotton wick, insert it in the plastic tube, and you have on-the-go aromatherapy. To use an inhaler, simply hold it close to your nose and breathe in. Do not stick the inhaler into your nose.

ESSENTIAL TAKE CARE TIP

#54 Check Your Bedding

Take care of you by keeping your space in bed as comfortable as possible. One study I found showed that 47% of people lose valuable sleep – up to three hours a week – because the person they're sleeping with is tossing and turning. Protect your territory! A bed that's big enough and stable enough will allow you to sleep the way you want to without feeling everything that's happening on the other side.

Maybe it's time to get a new bed. Take a few minutes to think about where you're sleeping. Ask yourself: Is it large enough for you both to stretch out and get comfortable? Do you wake up feeling sore? There are so many new kinds of mattresses and pillows now. If you haven't been bed shopping in a while, you may be surprised with how high-tech the industry has become. Companies do their own research to create products to address their customers' needs. If you're a side sleeper for example, you'll be able to find a mattress and a pillow that supports your style. Same for back and stomach sleepers.

Really look at your bedding, too. You work hard and you spend a big part of your life in bed. You deserve soft sheets and blankets that wrap you up in comfort every night. There's nothing like high quality cotton and down – or even silk! - to make you feel like curling up and dreaming. Remember, quality sleep is not a luxury, it's a necessity every bit as important as good nutrition and physical activity to our overall health.

LINEN SPRAY RECIPE

Ingredients

7-12 Lavender

4 oz glass spray bottle

3 oz Witch Hazel or Vodka (either will help to keep the Essential Oils distributed. They also dry faster than water to help protect your fabrics from any moisture. Spray a little on an area you won't be able to see and let it dry to make sure it doesn't discolor your bedding).

Method

Add the Witch Hazel or vodka to the spray bottle, then add your Essential Oils, shake, and mist over bedding to help create the environment you'd like. Some people like to add a single Oil to their sprays, others like blends.

There are hundreds of linen spray recipes that cover a variety of scents. One of my favorites is:

3 Douglas Fir Essential Oil

3 Grapefruit Essential Oil

3 Juniper Berry Essential Oil

It's an interesting, fresh, outdoorsy scen[t] that's not too heavy. It can be calming, but provide positive energy at the same time. These sprays make beautiful gifts.

A FEW MORE IMPORTANT THOUGHTS ABOUT SLEEP

Remember in Chapter 1 when I mentioned that caregivers are twice as likely to develop depression? Sometimes, not being able to sleep is a symptom of a bigger medical or emotional issue, like depression. Please, please, please, if you're having a lot of trouble sleeping and you think it's possible you're depressed, get to a doctor and talk about it. Depression is a medical issue like any other, and nothing to feel ashamed of…or ignore.

And, if none of the tips in this chapter seem to make a difference in your quality of sleep, I suggest you talk to a doctor about the possibility of sleep apnea. People with sleep apnea experience shallow breathing, or even stop breathing off and on during sleep. It can be caused by a collapsed airway. If you had this kind of sleep apnea, someone around you may have complained about your loud snoring (snoring doesn't always mean you've got sleep apnea, but it is one of the symptoms). Another, less common, form occurs when your brain sends the wrong signals to the muscles that control your breathing. About ten percent of the population has been diagnosed with the condition, but medical researchers think that many, many more people are walking around with undiagnosed sleep apnea.

A variety of effective treatments are available, but of course, those treatments can only be offered if there's a diagnosis.

A good laugh and a long sleep are the best cures in the doctor's book.

- Irish Proverb

Self-care starts with making a commitment to being gentle with yourself. Would you talk to others that way you talk to yourself? Give yourself credit for the tough work you're doing. The more you take a moment to appreciate yourself, the better you'll be able to move away from a harsh, critical inner voice.

CHAPTER SIX

Clean Yourself Up

When I'm out speaking to groups, many of the caregivers I meet tell me that their daily beauty routine -- if they're lucky -- consists of brushing their teeth and splashing some water on their face. If they get to any makeup, it's whatever they can find in the bottom of their purse and apply in the rearview mirror at stoplights.

I understand this! So, this chapter isn't about glamour girl advice. It's about understanding that how you feel about your appearance also connects to larger issues of self-confidence and self-esteem. These things play a big role in your overall well-being.

Putting ourselves last means that our appearance suffers too. You know that how you feel on the inside affects the way you look on the outside; and the reverse is true as well.

When you're looking rumpled and rundown, chances are good that you will be feeling rumpled and rundown. That's not how I want you to feel!

Mostly, I just want you to know that it's OK to care about what you see in the mirror, and I want to help you feel happier about the person looking back at you. It may be tough to think about a little pampering as a priority, with so many other "more important" things to take care of, but taking care of ourselves in this way is important too.

At one time or another, we probably all have felt a need to retreat. Recognizing that need, spas and medical spas continue to be an emerging trend. In fact, the business of wellness is one of the fastest growing industries today.

Spas are in the business of helping people relax, and they do this by focusing on stress management, aromatherapy, and wellness. Aromatherapy, the power of scent, and the many benefits of Essential Oils themselves are increasingly being used for their strong therapeutic qualities. We can use Essentials Oils to help us feel good inside and out with some easy, inexpensive, non-toxic products for a home spa experience.

First, let's go over some major benefits of pampering and relaxation:

- It protects your heart.
- It lowers your risk of catching a cold.
- It boosts your memory.
- It lowers your stroke risk.
- It reduces your risk of depression.
- It helps you make better decisions.
- It supports weight management.
- It reduces acne.
- It supports your relationships.
- It reduces your risk of all major disease.

A little attention to the outside revitalizes us on the inside. I believe that God gave us these amazing bodies with a charge to take care of them. When we treat our bodies with respect, we enjoy many wonderful results:

PHYSICALLY

Taking a nice bath isn't going to strengthen your heart the way a walk will, any more than brushing your hair will take the place of a few minutes with a Fitness Band to help your triceps. However, some time in the tub can help you to relax and keep your stress levels in check. That's what we're after right now.

When you're relaxed, important physical things begin to happen. Your body and brain don't sense any threats (that's basically what stress is – our animal-like reaction to threats), and your nervous system, heart rate, blood pressure and digestive systems all regulate to normal levels. All that from a little bath? Yes! Or a shoulder massage… or a facial treatment..or a foot rub! – whatever it is that makes you think "mmmm…" they all trigger the same system-balancing physical responses in your body.

EMOTIONALLY

When you make time to slip away for a bath, manicure or massage, you send a clear message to others (and to you) that you are worth taking care of too. Also, when you give some attention to your appearance, others will notice. If it just so happens that you get a few compliments for your efforts, then enjoy it! Those little affirming moments will fuel you, filling up your depleted tank with confidence and well-being.

Successful programs like Dress for Success realize this. They give women who've come through tough situations new clothes and coaching on appearance, and they've seen positive and powerful results! Their clients look better, feel better, and go on to get new jobs and start new lives. These women recognize that low self-esteem can make you miss opportunities because you're afraid to take them. If you don't have confidence in your worth, you won't speak up for yourself, and you won't have much of a chance at getting what you want.

Any act of caring for yourself is empowering and uplifting, and it sends a great message to your brain. Your brain can actually get in the habit of being depressed, but doing something just for you on a regular basis can help train your brain to be happy again. Take just a few minutes to make sure you leave the house projecting an image you are comfortable with---and that's key – this isn't about what society says you should look like, but what feels right to you. Doing this allows you to face your day in a more positive frame of mind, feeling competent and ready for any challenges that may come your way.

This kind of self-care can also help to chip away at feelings of resentment or anger you may have about your caregiving situation -- the time it's taking, the energy it's draining, and that constant nagging question, why is it always me all the time? Those feelings can creep in quietly and grow quickly. We don't always want to admit it, but it's common to become upset or even angry at the person (or people) we're caring for because of all the stress that's building up. A little self-pampering can go a long way to keeping the internal peace by preventing those kinds of feelings from taking over. We each have our own special beauty and value -- wouldn't it be nice to get in touch with that again? Think of the time you're spending on you as strength training for your self-esteem. A little bit, a few times a week, and soon you'll find that you're feeling pretty darned good.

YOUR APPEARANCE MATTERS TO OTHERS, TOO

You may feel it's kind of shallow, but without a doubt, appearance matters in so many aspects of our culture. Several studies have shown that when people are perceived as pulled together and attractive they are usually treated with more attention and respect in a variety of settings and situations.

Research from Princeton psychologists shows all it takes is a tenth of a second for us to start forming opinions about a person! Whew! That doesn't give us much time to make a good impression. I've also read that only about seven percent of what we communicate to one another is in words. The rest is all conveyed through our appearance, voice, expressions and body language. If this is so, then you can see how taking care of how you present yourself to others can greatly improve the way you interact with them.

If how we look wasn't so linked to feeling good, and even achieving success, we wouldn't be spending billions of dollars a year on lotions, potions, injections, extensions, and implants to improve our appearance. You and I know that there's no miracle potion or instant glamour-in-a-syringe. Looking good can actually be a lot simpler than that: It's about taking care of ourselves and then projecting that happy, confident feeling as we move through our day.

IT STARTS WHEN WE'RE BABIES

We want approval. We want to fit in. We want people to like us. Behavioral Science studies tell us that these issues are truly critical in our development. If these needs are not met in childhood, body image problems often follow us into adulthood.

A Psychology Today study showed that 56 percent of women and 43 percent of men who took part said they were unhappy with their appearance. A British survey of 3,500 women showed that two out of three women either have mixed feelings or feel depressed when they see themselves naked! These statistics are sad because if we are not happy with ourselves, it's tough to be happy with life.

THE ESSENTIAL BENEFITS

Essential Oils have long been considered extremely powerful, especially for beauty and wellness. Ancient Egyptian, Greek and Roman women and men used Oils in a variety of routines and rituals for skin and hair care.

Although there's been a growing demand for natural products, the vast majority of modern, expensive personal care items are filled with harmful chemicals. We know that what we put on our skin doesn't necessarily stay there. Our skin acts as a protective barrier, but it's also extremely porous. Chemicals in the products we use can enter our blood stream, tissues, and organs through our skin, as well as by breathing in their scents.

Women are exposed to more chemicals than men because they use more personal care products, but studies show that anyone near these products can also be affected. People who test these things have found that the environmental toxins contained in beauty products are often endocrine disruptors, which means they can block hormones and hormone production. The toxins can also cause problems for the trillions of bacteria in our guts working hard to keep us healthy, and be dangerous for the systems that create energy for every cell in our body. Could the synthetic products you're using be leaving you feeling tired, hungry and sick? Yes!

The great news is, as we're getting smarter about taking care of ourselves in a healthy way, it's getting easier to say no to the toxic stuff, and make more conscious purchases, or just make our own natural care products.

Are you with me? Great! If you're ready to devote some time to taking care of your appearance, I want a commitment from you that you'll do what it takes to bring out the beautiful person that you are. Think of your pampering time as a little vacation from the stress you carry around every day. These 10-minute tips for appearance are your ticket to a happier brain…and body.

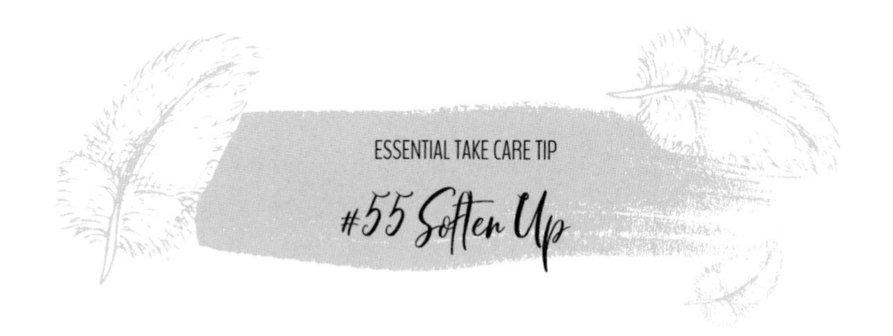

Stress, dehydration, and lack of sleep make our skin prone to dryness and roughness. Soften up with a homemade citrus-sugar scrub. In this quick and easy double-punch treatment, citric acid works to soften and loosen dry skin flakes, then the sugar scrub removes them, letting the healthy skin underneath shine through. Visit me at www.TakeCareTips.com for videos with hints and tips of how to make scrubs and other pampering products!

ESSENTIAL SUGAR SCRUB

Ingredients	Method
12 Wild Orange Essential Oil 3/4 cup White Sugar 1/2 cup Olive Oil (Fractionated Coconut Oil or Almond Oil work well, too) Small Glass Jar (optional)	In a small bowl, combine all the ingredients, and stir to blend. Scoop a little out and massage into cuticles, heels, elbows, knees...any rough spots. You can make this in greater quantity and store in a small jar. Since this blend contains a citrus Oil, it is advised, due to photosensitivity, not to expose the area of the skin that citrus Oils have been applied to, for at least 12 hours after application. BONUS BENEFIT: The citrus scent will give you a mood and energy boost!

ESSENTIAL TAKE CARE TIP

#56 The Eyes Have It

They say the eyes are the windows to the soul. Eyes are the first thing we notice about someone's face. Are yours looking tired? Brighten up your eye area with this homemade roller ball blend of Essential Oils:

BRIGHT EYES BLEND

Ingredients	Method
5 Frankincense Essential Oil 5 Lavender Essential Oil 5 Lemon Essential Oil 10 ml Rollerball Bottle	Add the Oils to a 10ml rollerball bottle, and top with Fractionated Coconut Oil. Gently apply a dab beneath each eye morning and night, being careful not to get any in your eyes. Since this blend contains a citrus oil, it is advised, due to photosensitivity, not to expose the area of the skin that citrus Oils have been applied to, for at least 12 hours after application.

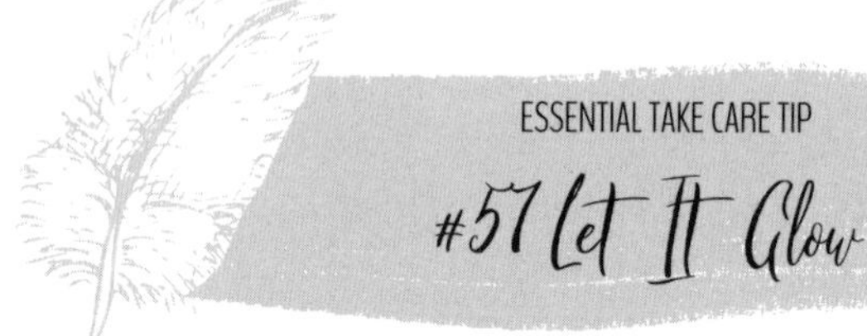

When we're rundown, our skin can take on a dull appearance. It can make us look older than we are! Here's a blend to bring back a healthy glow that will stay with you all day long:

GLOW BLEND

Ingredients		Method
5	Lavender Essential Oil	Add Oils to an empty 10ml rollerball bottle, top with Fractionated Coconut Oil. Apply across your face, avoiding the eye area using your fingers, or swipe the blend across a cotton ball or cotton pad, and apply.
5	Cedarwood Essential Oil	
5	Tea Tree Essential Oil	
Fractionated Coconut Oil		
10 ml Rollerball Bottle		

ESSENTIAL TAKE CARE TIP

#58 Plump It Up

Full lips help make you look healthier and younger. There are a bunch of lip boosting products out there, but why not try this non-toxic solution?

Mix a little bit of honey with sugar and a drop of Wild Orange Essential Oil, or any citrus Oil, to create an exfoliating treatment that will soften dry lips and give them a healthy glow. Just massage on and tissue off. You can pre-mix this in a bigger quantity and store it in a little glass jar for about a week, so it's ready to go when you are.

ESSENTIAL TAKE CARE TIP

#59 The Multi-Tasking Bath

A great way to start with any self-care routine is by carving out some tub time. The benefits of allowing ourselves to relax in warm water have been studied for a long time, and from a medical standpoint, a bath is good for our heart, lungs, brain, immune system, nervous system, and even hormone levels.

Adding Essential Oils and Epsom Salt to your bath enhances feelings of soaking away the stress of the day. Epsom salt is also known as magnesium sulfate. And some believe the magnesium provides a variety of health benefits. Several studies on some of the specific wellness claims for Epsom Salt are inconclusive, but people who use it swear it soothes sore muscles and makes them feel more relaxed. You can find Epsom salts online and in the pharmacy or cosmetic area of most stores.

SOOTHING BODY BATH SALTS

Ingredients

- 2 Frankincense Essential Oil
- 2 Lavender Essential Oil
- 2 Marjoram Essential Oil
- 2 cups Epsom Salt
- 1 cup Baking Soda
- Mason jar or other glass jar

Method

Mix all ingredients together until blended, and pour into a glass jar (a small Mason jar works well). Add a quarter cup to your bath as you're filling the tub with warm water. The salts will dissolve, but your bath will be beautifully scented. Climb in the tub and soak for 10-20 minutes for an aromatic, soothing experience.

ESSENTIAL TAKE CARE TIP

#60 Take It Off…And More

There are so many great uses for coconut oil, and one way I put my Fractionated Coconut Oil to work is as my make-up remover. A little massaged into your face gently works to dissolve all make-up---including mascara! If it worked for my TV makeup---it will work for you---trust me!

I don't stop there with my Fractionated Coconut Oil though, it's a great primer---just pat a little on your face before make-up for a smooth application, and follow up with a dab after for a dewy glow. It's great to use on the delicate skin under your eyes, and as a lip moisturizer, too.

How many products could you get rid of by replacing them with your one bottle of Fractionated Coconut Oil? Simplifying your self-care feels good!

ESSENTIAL TAKE CARE TIP

#61 Love Your Belly

If you've had children, or, if you're someone who hasn't taken the best care of yourself, your belly might not be something you think about with feelings of pride. What a great place to start on a path to loving your WHOLE self…bumps, bruises, stretchmarks, and all. A little bit at a time, and soon you'll be feeling more self-assured, and comfortable with yourself. My sweet friend Jen Frey is a living example of this. She's gone from a stay-at-home, homeschooling momma, to a top health and wellness company leader, and runs a huge organization from home. Jen's mission is to empower every woman to be confident and care for her family in a natural way, "I want to help women find their purpose in life by stretching out of their comfort zone and growing into the beautiful women they were meant to be," Jen told me.

Here's a tip from Jen to help you feel stronger from your core!

BEAUTIFUL BELLY TIP

"For those of us that have had babies, we know the struggle is real when it comes to skin that was stretched way too far. The skin doesn't bounce back after it's made room for those precious little ones growing inside of us," Jen says.

Jen uses a micro roller 4-5 times a week on her abdomen. She follows that up with a layer of a pre-made blend of Yarrow|Pomegranate Seed Oil, which is known for its calming properties, as well as for numerous anti-aging benefits for the skin. A micro roller, sometimes called a micro derma roller, is a little hand-hand wand with a roller on it that has little sharp threads. As you roll it over your skin, it agitates the surface, which is said to stimulate skin repair and cell regeneration. She also mixes Rose Oil and Sandalwood with a tightening serum and massages that into her skin on the days she doesn't use her micro roller. "This combination helps the appearance of my skin drastically," Jen says. Find out more about these pre-made health and beauty blends at www.TakeCareTips.com

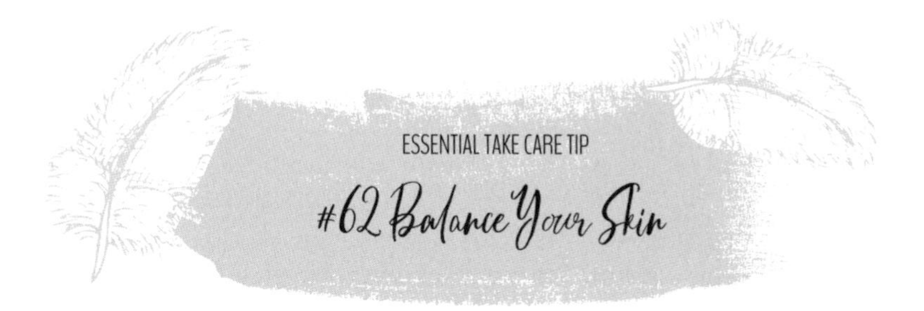

A change of seasons, stress levels, and more can cause our skin to be more oily or dry than normal. A toner helps to bring balance, as well as tone the skin and tighten pores. Many toners on the market contain chemicals---why spray that on your face, when you can make something natural at home...and you only need a few drops of Essential Oil, so this is a budget-friendly alternative as well! Ancient Egyptians loved to use Geranium Oil for beautiful, glowing skin and hair. You'll find Geranium is a versatile Oil. It's also said to reduce feelings of stress.

GERANIUM FACE MIST

Ingredients

8 Geranium Essential Oil

4 Tbsp Water

2 Tbsp Witch Hazel

4 oz Spray Bottle

Method

Add all ingredients to the spray bottle, shake, and mist your face, or for a heavier application, spray onto a cotton ball, and gently wipe across a clean face.

Bonus Tip! While you have your Geranium Oil out, add a few drops to your shampoo or conditioner to give your hair a healthy-looking boost!

ESSENTIAL TAKE CARE TIP

#63 Take Care Of Your Caring Hands

Take care of those hands that do so much for others by spending just a little time to give them some love. A hand massage with a squeeze of Fractionated Coconut Oil or unscented lotion and a drop or two of Lavender Essential Oil goes a long way towards soothing and moisturizing your hands, and calming your brain, as you breathe in the beautiful scent.

To focus on the nails, here's a powerhouse blend I like to make in a 10ml roller ball bottle, which makes it easy to roll across nails, then massage it into the nail beds and cuticles.

NAILED IT BLEND

Ingredients

- 4 Lavender Essential Oil
- 4 Lemon Essential Oil
- 4 Frankincense Essential Oil
- 4 Myrrh Essential Oil
- 10 ml Rollerball Bottle
- Vitamin E Oil

Method

Add Essential Oils to a 10ml roller ball bottle, top with Vitamin E Oil. To use, roll across nails, then go back and massage the blend into each nail and cuticle area. Your nails will instantly look and feel better!

This blend contains a citrus Oil. It is advised, due to photosensitivity, not to expose the area of the skin that citrus Oils have been applied to, for at least 12 hours after application.

Vitamin E – strengthens brittle nails, softens cuticles, helps prevent hangnails, and conditions cuticles

Lavender– calms and soothes inflamed cuticles and strengthens weak, brittle nails

Myrrh– one of the best essential oils for nail growth. Moisturizes deeply to help relieve brittleness, thinning, and breaking

Frankincense– helps moisturize nails so that they can grow longer and stronger and enhances the properties of the other Essential Oils

Lemon – helps strengthen damaged and peeling nails

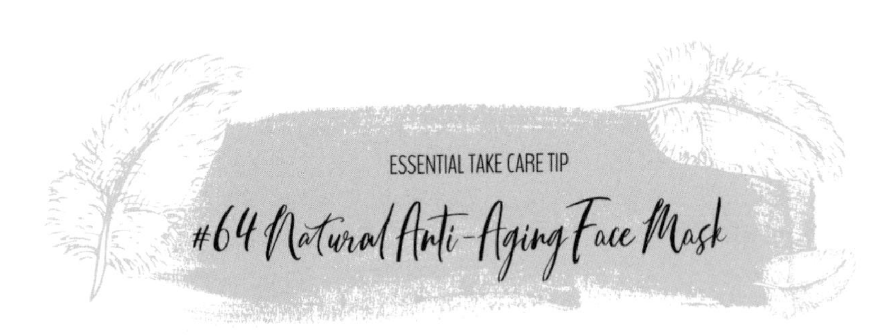

ESSENTIAL TAKE CARE TIP

#64 Natural Anti-Aging Face Mask

Show your face some love with this at-home spa treatment. This natural mask is so easy to make – and you only need two ingredients! Use this mask once a week to see an improvement in your skin quality and appearance.

NATURAL ANTI-AGING FACE MASK

Ingredients	Method
1 Tbsp Baking Soda 2 Tbsp Liquid Coconut Oil	In a small bowl, mix the Baking Soda and Coconut Oil together until it becomes a well-blended paste. Gently apply to the face, concentrating on areas where you're seeing fine lines and wrinkles (the forehead, around the eyes, near the lips). Massage the mixture into those areas, then leave it on your face and relax for five minutes. Rinse your face with warm water, and pat dry.

Age is inevitable.

Aging isn't

- Marv Levy

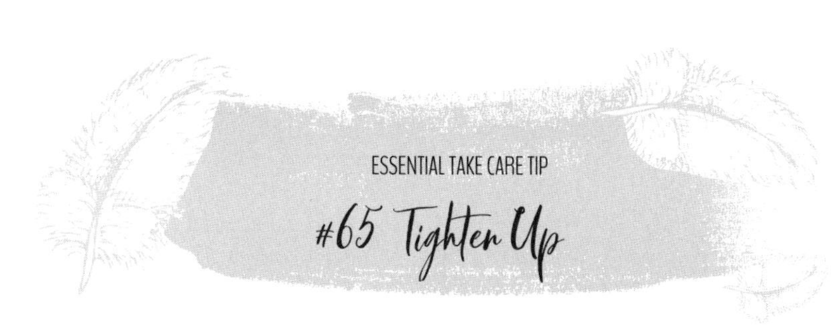

ESSENTIAL TAKE CARE TIP

#65 Tighten Up

Saggy skin is a part of life! To boost your confidence and help firm things up, try this recipe. The Oils featured in this blend are known to help with tightening pores, improving skin tone and elasticity, and reducing crepey skin. They are also said to help reduce inflammation. Make it and store it in a bottle with a dropper top to make it easy to apply. This one smells great, too!

TIGHTEN UP BLEND

Ingredients		Method
4	Peppermint Essential Oil	Add the Essential Oils to a dropper top bottle, fill the rest of the way with Fractionated Coconut Oil. Massage a few drops into your skin ---think thighs, arms, neck...
4	Lime Essential Oil	
4	Grapefruit Essential Oil	This blend contains a citrus Oil. It is advised, due to photosensitivity, not to expose the area of the skin that citrus Oils have been applied to, for at least 12 hours after application.
Fractionated Coconut Oil		

ESSENTIAL TAKE CARE TIP

#66 Hair Essentials

Over-washing your hair, using harsh shampoos and styling products, heated styling tools, chemical treatments, and exposure to the sun can also strip away our hair's natural oils, leaving our hair dry and more prone to damage. Stress, aging, and some medications can also cause us to lose hair.

Besides washing your hair less, using a good natural shampoo and conditioner, and avoiding hair products that contain alcohol; you can use Essential Oils to improve scalp and hair health. Simply massaging a little jojoba or coconut oil into your scalp can make a difference. Try this deep conditioner for soft and smooth hair:

ESSENTIAL DEEP CONDITIONER

Ingredients

- 4 Lavender Essential Oil
- 2 Rosemary Essential Oil
- 2 Geranium Essential Oil
- 1 Tea Tree Essential Oil
- 3 tablespoons solid coconut oil
- 1 tablespoon olive oil

Method

Add coconut oil, olive oil, and the Essential Oils in a mixing bowl. Using a hand mixer on medium/high speed, blend until you get a thick, whipped creamy consistency. To use, apply to clean, dry hair, and comb through to distribute evenly. Relax for 10 minutes, then rinse, shampoo, condition, and style. Use as needed to maintain healthy hair. Visit me at www.TakeCareTips.com for video tutorials on how to make your own natural hair care products!

ESSENTIAL TAKE CARE TIP

#67 Vein, Vein Go Away

Many spider veins and varicose veins are caused when valves in our veins become weak, or have been damaged. It causes a backup of blood that pools there instead of traveling back to the heart. Other things can cause spider veins too, though: hormone issues, exposure to the sun, and injuries. Spider veins are often found to be superficial, cosmetic situations, and can be treated in a variety of ways. To be safe, I encourage you to check with a vein specialist to make sure your spider veins are not related to hidden varicose veins, which can show up as a bulging vein, along with a feeling of pain, heaviness, or intense tingling. That being said, Essential Oils have been found to have properties that can support healthy veins.

Here's a blend you can make that features Essential Oils that will help your circulation, and more:

CIRCULATION SUPPORT BLEND

Ingredients

3 Lemongrass Essential Oil
said to dilute blood vessels and promote health circulation

1 Lemon Essential Oil
stringent and anti-inflammatory; helps to soothe

3 Lavender Essential Oil
soothes aches and pains, and reduces inflammation

5 Cypress Essential Oil
can strengthen the veins, and supports lymphatic drainage

3 Helichrysum Essential Oil
an anti-inflammatory that calms and supports healthy blood flow

10ml Rollerball Bottle

Fractionated Coconut Oil or Almond Oil

Method

Add Essential Oils to a 10ml roller ball bottle, fill the rest of the way with Coconut or Almond Oil. Roll on legs and gently massage into the skin.

This blend contains a citrus Oil. It is advised, due to photosensitivity, not to expose the area of the skin that citrus Oils have been applied to, for at least 12 hours after application.

ESSENTIAL TAKE CARE TIP

#68 Bedtime Foot Rub

We don't really think about it, but our feet really serve us well throughout our busy day. Massaging the feet has been shown to calm the body and mind, reduce anxious feelings, support healthy circulation, and improve the quality of your sleep. Massage is considered one of the oldest healing arts. Add Essential Oils to that ancient practice to enhance the benefits. Here's an easy massage lotion you can make and start using tonight!

BEDTIME FOOT RUB LOTION

Ingredients

- 5 Lavender Essential Oil
- 5 Wild Orange Essential Oil
- 3 Frankincense Essential Oil
- 2 Peppermint Essential Oil

1 cup solid coconut oil

Method

Add all ingredients to a small bowl, and whisk to combine. Store in a glass jar, and keep it on your nightstand, so you'll remember to use it as part of your bedtime routine.

This blend contains a citrus Oil. It is advised, due to photosensitivity, not to expose the area of the skin that citrus Oils have been applied to, for at least 12 hours after application.

CHAPTER SEVEN

Get That Mess Cleaned up

In a lot of ways, our homes are extensions of ourselves. They are our most personal environments. With this in mind, doesn't it make sense that your home should be your sanctuary…your retreat…your safe zone? It should not only provide physical shelter, but emotional shelter and support for you and your family, all of your habits, loveable quirks and individual needs.

If your home is in a state of chaos, with stuff on every surface and closets like black holes, then your home is no longer doing its job for you. You don't have time to sort through piles of papers looking for the slip from the doctor that you brought home a month ago. You don't need to walk into your kitchen, take one look at the sink, and give a heavy sigh. Your days are crazy enough – why add to the stress?

When your home and your schedule are disorganized, your health and your overall quality of life suffer:

- When we're not able to find what we need, it causes stress ("Where the heck are my keys?!?").
- When we're surrounded by things we don't need we feel unsettled, overwhelmed and out of control.
- It's hard to feel optimistic or motivated when your surroundings are cluttered.
- It's hard to think clearly with confusion and clutter all around you.
- Lots of clutter in high-traffic areas increases the risk of someone getting hurt.

You know that clutter in your home doesn't look good, feel good, or make life any easier. When you're trying to manage your own life as well as someone else's, you need to be organized and efficient to the extreme. It's really about taking control. Together, let's get control of your time and space. Let's try to fill each only with things that are helpful and healthy. Sound impossible right now? Stick with me…

LET'S TALK CLUTTER

Have you ever watched any of those home makeover shows where a crew goes in and helps a family reclaim a room in their home simply by bulldozing out all of the junk that's in it? I love them - not just for how pretty the rooms look afterward, but for how wonderful the people say they feel after going through a decluttering process.

When I watch, I pay special attention to the interviews the hosts do with the people about why and how their rooms got to be so messy in the first place. All the answers seem to have not only a time component, but an emotional one as well.

These people say they don't have time to create an organizational system for their home, and that it's hard for them to let go of a lot of the things that are cluttering up their space. Once the chaos has set in, they are totally overwhelmed and don't know where or how to begin.

You don't need to hire a bulldozer (though it might seem like that's the only thing that will help), but I do want you to begin just by looking around your space – perhaps the room you're in right now. As you go about your day, opening drawers and looking for stuff on your desk, pick up a random thing and ask yourself:

- Do I actually use it?
- Does this bring me joy?

"It's about choosing joy," says Marie Kondo, Tidying Expert, and host of her own Netflix series, '*Tidying up with Marie Kondo.*' Her New York Times best-selling book, "The Life Changing Magic of Tidying Up" teaches people that properly simplifying and organizing your home once means you'll never have to do it again. How do you "properly" simplify and organize your home? Kondo's plan is trademarked as '*The KonMari Method™*', and includes six basic steps: commit yourself to tidying up, imagine your ideal lifestyle, finish discarding first, tidy by category not location, follow the right order, and ask yourself if it sparks joy.

Kondo's system for clutter-busting attacks physical and emotional excess, and although the process can seem overwhelming at times, the dreamy end goal that keeps you going is the thought of living in a house that contains only the things you really use, and make you smile.

Keeping and working around things that you don't need or want because you feel obligated to (it was a gift), or you just don't feel you have time to deal with it, drains your brain power, your time and your energy. While it may seem daunting at first, getting rid of some of that clutter can change your life by replacing negative energy with positive energy. A clean space represents hope and possibility, and allows you to see clearly what you are able to accomplish.

To get organized and really make it last, and to make your home a warm and happy place, stop thinking in terms of throwing things away; rather, seek to use the things you have to their best, practical purposes. If you don't need them, you're not helping anyone by keeping them in your space. It will take a little time to create a system that works for you, because the process of living keeps potential clutter coming. There will be mail in the mailbox most days. The kids will get new toys. You'll get new clothes. You'll receive gifts. You'll take on new projects that have a lot of paperwork attached. But once you get that system in place, you will be able to welcome and manage all of it in a controlled, confident way – and you'll save a LOT of time.

THE TRANSITION-CLUTTER CONNECTION

Have you ever thought about how major life transitions are marked by parting with things from the past that we don't need now? When a new baby is coming home, a space is cleared to welcome him; when you change jobs you clear out your desk; when you get married, you both get rid of enough stuff so you can – somehow – share a closet and a home; and at death, everything is cleared except only the most valuable tokens to those left behind.

During each of these transitions, while the material changes are going on outside, emotional changes are going on inside. Remembering that you are creating emotional space as well as physical space makes these major transitions less stressful, and allows you room to contemplate exciting possibilities for the future.

On a lighter note, when you decide to invest the time you need to bring order to your home, you may feel like you've lost weight! And you don't have to cut any carbs. You are, quite literally, lightening the load and freeing your energy for the other things you want in your life. What a great feeling!

HOW DID ALL OF THIS JUNK GET HERE?

Even professional organizers have days and weeks when they are unorganized. Many things can bring clutter and chaos into your life, and caregiving is certainly one of them. Dropping everything to take care of a family member means that daily life maintenance often gets pushed down the priority list. If you're feeling sick, depressed or overworked, you might feel too tired to keep up with the housework. This is how kitchens seem to explode overnight. Throw in holidays, unexpected guests, extra projects at work, school functions and meetings, and your days are full of potential roadblocks to organization.

Professional organizers and psychologists have identified and categorized several reasons why clutter can build up. They include:

- Trauma – something important happens that causes you to drop everything else you were working on.

- Stress/Depression – you are so unhappy with your life that you can't see your way clear to do anything to improve it, so you give up.
- Perceived Lack of Time – you feel you are just too busy to devote any time to a big home project. You don't think you even have the time to figure out where to start.

My experience has been that clutter is kind of a slow, sneaky threat. And – this is not an easy thing to come to grips with – it's been found that the amount of clutter in your home is related to the amount of clutter in your brain.

A professional organizer friend of mine puts it this way: "Clutter represents unmade decisions." Thinking about that has actually made my stomach hurt as I've looked around at the stacks of papers on my kitchen desk (and table, and counter, if we're really being honest with each other here). Clutter represents unmade decisions – yep, makes me queasy. An overwhelming feeling sets in: "How will I ever find the brain power I'll need to make all the decisions needed to get rid of that stack of paper?" And, because it seems too intimidating, nothing gets done. But the stack of papers doesn't just sit there – it grows! Other people in the house start to think, "This must be the place for papers." So school forms get mixed in with mail, which gets mixed in with medical information, and it all starts looking really, really frightening.

If you know you have a clutter problem and you honestly can't imagine how you'll find the time or energy to fix it, just breathe for a sec. Then believe me when I say you CAN dig your way out, a little bit at a time.

As a family caregiver, there are many times where you feel that things are out of your control. This is one opportunity for you to have absolute control. Jump on it! The secret to being organized, for life, starts with taking time right now to make some decisions about how you're going to set up a system that works for you.

ORGANIZING BASICS

Starting with any room you choose, walk in and pretend that you're in a home that you've rented for vacation. What does the room look like? Does it seem like you could easily find everything you need? What does/doesn't meet with your approval?

Do you want your money back so that you can run someplace else?

When you realize you can't leave, because this is your home, think about the room in terms of efficiency first. Is it functional? Are you making the best use of the space?

Problem areas will stand out. Is there a pile of toys on the floor? A stack of mail on the counter? Those are the places that are screaming for some organizational help. Start with these easily identifiable areas, and decide on a fix that is easy to maintain. Taking care of those kinds of glaring trouble spots can be pretty quick and easy.

Work with them. You're not going for perfection here, but just getting a little more control of the space. For example, if that's where the kids always play with their toys, trying to move their whole play area could be a real pain. So let the space stay as-is for play, but corral those toys in a big bin or laundry basket so that they have a home other than the floor – and then establish a new family rule; toys into the basket. Walk into any preschool. Those teachers run a tight ship! This kind of a system works there. It can work at home, too.

If your kitchen counter seems to be the most comfortable resting place for the mail, so be it, but place a basket or wooden tray on the counter to keep those letters contained.

Move around your home like that, staying focused on working with the obvious problems first. Yes, you are the one having to invest the time and energy to do the initial decision making, but once your systems are in place, everybody else in the house will know them and can use them! In the long run, this process will save you time.

Setting up an organization system also teaches the children in your house important life skills. It teaches them independence, because with all of their toys organized, kids will feel empowered around making decisions about their toys and other things as well. It teaches them responsibility, because they are helping to care for the home by putting things where they belong. It teaches them to respect the value of things, because they are able to put them in a special place rather than just toss them on the floor. Perhaps you can even involve them in the process and see what ideas they have for a system – they will be more likely to use it if they feel like they helped create it.

HOW ESSENTIAL OILS CAN HELP

Clearing things out of our physical space can stir up quite a bit in our emotional space:

- Our attachment to material things, versus people or experiences.
- Some anxiety when we think about throwing away or donating things.
- Feelings of overwhelm when we think of how much work has to be done.

Using Essential Oils as part of your clearing process will help you be gentle with yourself as you work through this.

REMEMBER...ROME WASN'T BUILT IN A DAY

If you have a lot of clutter clearing to do, thinking about all of it at once can make you nuts. Focus instead on keeping everything in perspective. You will feel better if you get your desk cleaned off, but the world won't end if it doesn't happen this minute. If an area seems too big to deal with, or requires too many decisions right now, go smaller. For those of you who look at that heap in the closet or the sky-high pile of papers and bills on the dining table and wonder how you'll ever make it go away, this is the key. You don't need to conquer it all at once.

You can start with just one Essential Take Care Tip. Allow the results to sink in, and allow yourself some time to appreciate the progress you've made. Slow and steady will help you win this battle once and for all.

Need some help gearing up to do this kind of work? My friend Vivien Garside developed this blend. She's a caregiver to her mom, and has fostered over 40 children so she has vast experience of caregiving. She, and her family, run a successful Essential Oil Supplies company based in the UK - www.eosupplies.com. Viv says this blend helps her when she wants to "hit the floor and clear the decks!"

Use this to help focus the mind and center the emotions to get you ready for a clutter clearing session.

CLEAR THE DECK ROLLERBALL BLEND

Ingredients

- 3 Lemon Essential Oil
- 3 Lemongrass Essential Oil
- 2 Lime Essential Oil
- 2 Siberian Fir Essential Oil
- 1 Arborvitae Essential Oil
- 1 Cinnamon Bark Essential Oil

10 ml Rollerball Bottle

Fractionated Coconut Oil

Method

Add all Oils to a 10 ml Rollerball Bottle. Top with Fractionated Coconut Oil. Roll on pulse points, and breathe in the scent to experience the benefits.

This blend contains a citrus Oil. It is advised, due to photosensitivity, not to expose the area of the skin that citrus Oils have been applied to, for at least 12 hours after application.

ESSENTIAL TAKE CARE TIP

#69 One Thing At A Time

Attack your clutter by starting with the quick fixes; small spaces that are easy to spot. I'd like you to look around and think about what area in your home is bothering you the most. What causes the most frustration…trying to get ready for your busy day in a messy bathroom? Then spend your time there first. In a 10 minute chunk, whenever you can grab it, choose something there that you'd like to fix. Just one thing. In 10 minutes you can: clean off a vanity, move laundry to the washer, or go through your makeup drawer, for example. Take care of yourself first and don't get bogged down worrying about what you "should" do. Attacking the place that irritates you the most will help you the most. Keep this in mind no matter what organizing task you're working on.

It can be difficult to focus on just one thing when you feel like everywhere you look, there's something that needs your attention. Essential Oils can support us emotionally to help us stay focused. Using the Oils aromatically is great for this purpose. Set up your diffuser with this blend to create a motivating atmosphere.

ENERGIZE AND FOCUS DIFFUSER BLEND

Ingredients

- 2 Lemon Essential Oil
- 2 Peppermint Essential Oil
- 2 Rosemary Essential Oil

Method

Following the directions that come from the manufacturer, add Oils to your diffuser.

These Oils have been shown to support clarity, focus, and an upbeat energy. You'll love the scent!

ESSENTIAL TAKE CARE TIP

#10 Throw Ten Things Away

This tip came to me from a woman who watched my TV show. She says when she finds herself with a bonus 10 minutes, while dinner's cooking for example, she walks around the house and finds ten things to get rid of. Sometimes it's a book or two to donate, sometimes it's junk mail to shred and recycle. She says her little 10 minute de-cluttering sessions help her to feel like she's accomplished something, and getting rid of even a few extras keeps her on the right track for her bigger organizing projects. You can throw stuff in the trash, recycle it (bonus points), or keep a plastic bin handy for things you want to give away (extra bonus points). When it's full, drop the contents off at your local charity on your way to work, and then bring the empty bin back home to collect more giveaways.

Having a designated place (or plastic box) where you put things to give to charity, or items you just don't want anymore is liberating, too. No need to clutter the brain thinking where you're going to put the things you no longer want – take them right to that designated space, drop them in and move onto the next thing. When it's full donate the contents.

Lemongrass is an Oil you may know mostly from a flavoring in foods. Therapeutically, think of Lemongrass as an Essential Oil you can use to "let it go"! Diffusing a few drops of Lemongrass, or simply taking a few deep breaths of the Oil straight from the bottle as you get started with a decluttering session will help you quickly assess what you have and make decisions on what you can let go.

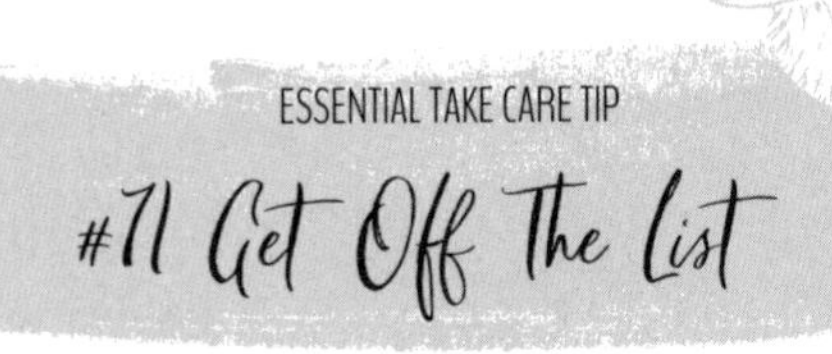

Over the course of our lives it's estimated that eight months are devoted to nothing but opening and dealing with junk mail. Every year the amount of junk mail sent out to homes equals more than 100 million trees! In response, forestry departments are planting more trees and communities are working with recycling companies to encourage environmental awareness programs. You can do your part by reducing the amount of junk mail that comes into your home.

You can start by going to www.DMAChoice.org and putting yourself on the Do Not Mail list. This is the website for the Mail Preference Service of the Direct Marketing Association; most companies that send out big volumes of mail refer to this list. Just fill out the online form.

You can get rid of most of those credit, mortgage and insurance offers by visiting www.OptOutPreScreen.com. This service is provided under the Fair Credit Reporting Act, which gives you the right to opt out of this kind of solicitation.

You will see a noticeable reduction in junk mail in your mailbox by doing those two fast, free things. Please note that it may take up to three months for you to be purged from all of the mailing cycles, so get the ball rolling now.

I hope you're feeling proud and accomplished as you move through these tips! These little actions are your path to big results. Celebrate the small steps by diffusing Bergamot Essential Oil. This is a personal favorite of mine. I love the spicy citrus scent so much I often wear it as perfume, and I always reach for it when I want to feel confident. Bergamot has a calming, yet uplifting quality, and from an emotional standpoint, this Oil supports feelings of self-love, self-worth, and self-acceptance. Go back and read that last sentence again. How beautiful would it be for you to feel those things about yourself? You deserve to---you're doing a great job!

ESSENTIAL TAKE CARE TIP

#72 Clear Your Desk

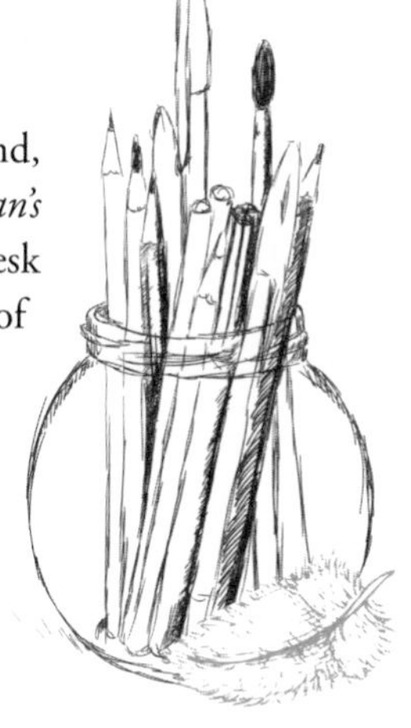

Do you have a built-in desk in your kitchen? My friend, lifestyle coach Mj Callaway, author of *The Frantic Woman's Guide to Feeding Family and Friends*, says that a kitchen desk can provide a nice, additional functional area in the heart of the home. But it's also kind of a danger zone, which can quickly become a mini-junkyard filled with everything from the kids' craft supplies to the daily mail. If you've got a desk that doubles as the family dump, Mary Jo says you can make it useful again by clearing it off in little ten-minute projects:

- Organize smaller office supplies like paper clips and clamps, rubber bands, push pins and so forth in a small multi-drawer organizer. These organizers come in various sizes with any number of pull-out drawers, and you can find them at most office supply, discount, craft or hardware stores. Once you've put everything into its proper place, label each drawer or container so that everyone knows where to find and store that stuff.

- Think about storing larger and bulkier items, like note pads, stapler and staples, and tape, in a three-drawer cart with attached wheels, so you can move it around easily. Find one that can easily fit under your desk to utilize wasted space. School supplies like crayons, markers, colored pencils, paints and glue can go there too.

- Afraid smaller pieces of paper with all those important notes will get lost in the shuffle? A recipe/index card box will keep them ready when you need them. Stick or staple the note to an index card, jot a key word at the top, and file.

- Have the kids go through their papers and art projects and separate them into piles. Scrapbook their favorites, or snap pictures to save in an online album. Shred the colored ones to line a gift basket. Re-purpose artwork as wrapping paper or book covers.

- When the desk is cleared off, make your own non-toxic, inexpensive surface spray to wipe it down.

ESSENTIAL SURFACE SPRAY

Ingredients

15 Lemon Essential Oil

15 Lavender Essential Oil

1 3/4 cups water

1/4 cup white vinegar

16 oz spray bottle

Method

Add all ingredients to the spray bottle. Shake, spray, and wipe clean.

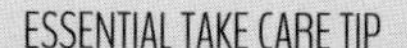

ESSENTIAL TAKE CARE TIP

#73 Mission Control

To make getting out the door much easier for you and everyone else in the morning, set up a control center for frequently used items. Find a space to keep your checkbook, some stamps and envelopes, a pen and pencil, pair of scissors, neutral-colored thread and a needle (or a little sewing kit), change and a few bills (for lunch and milk money), any tickets or parking tokens your family might use, etc. You can use one of those multi-drawer organizers, a hanging folder system, or anything that is easy to use and find things in.

For caregivers: I also recommend including a folder or notebook with all the important information you, or anyone else, may need related to the person you're taking care of - doctor's names and numbers, medications, and any medical instructions. Having the essentials all in one place is a huge time and sanity saver.

My friend Dr. Mariza Snyder is on a passionate mission to help put women back in control of their health. Her newest book *The Essential Oils Hormone Solution* quickly became a #1 National Best Seller.

"You matter. Your life matters. Your emotional health matters. Your hormonal balance matters. Your everything matters," she says. "You deserve to treat yourself with the same love and compassion that you dole out to the world."

This is one of Dr. Mariza's favorite Essential Oil blends to support an "I'm in control. I can do this" feeling all day long. It's one of those featured in her new book.

MOTIVATE AND RECHARGE ROLLERBALL BLEND

Ingredients

- **10** Wild Orange Essential Oil
- **10** Peppermint Essential Oil
- **7** Ylang Ylang Essential Oil
- **3** Basil Essential Oil
- 10 ml Rollerball Bottle
- Fractionated Coconut Oil

Method

Add the oils to a 10 ml rollerball bottle. Top off with Fractionated Coconut Oil or the carrier oil of your choice. Replace the rollerball top, and shake gently to combine. Roll on wrists, and behind the neck and ears. Inhale the aroma from your wrists as needed throughout the day for a healthy power boost. This blend contains a citrus Oil. It is advised, due to photosensitivity, not to expose the area of the skin that citrus Oils have been applied to, for at least 12 hours after application.

ESSENTIAL TAKE CARE TIP

#74 Mark Your Boundaries

Big picture, clutter management involves setting boundaries so that your schedule doesn't become cluttered as well. Think about things that zap your time on a regular basis and how you can put some tidy limits around them. One of the biggest schedule hogs is technology. Too many of us are slaves to our electronic gadgets. We feel the need to respond to every ding and beep instantly. If you added up all the time you spent on your phone, computer, and social media sites, you'd probably be pretty shocked with how much space you're giving it! How many of the 10 minute tips in this book could you put into action if you give yourself back some of that time? I have a few friends who are so happy with the break they've given themselves with boundaries around email: NO EMAIL ON WEEKENDS… or, NO EMAIL AFTER 5PM. They stick to that and it has allowed them to reclaim some time for themselves; it's also made their computer time more efficient. Take a few minutes to think of a personal policy you'd like to try, and tell the people you regularly correspond with what it is – chances are they'll think it's a great idea. Make technology work for your schedule instead of overwhelming it.

Another great way to do that is to take advantage of apps and settings that allow you to take control of the time you spend on technical distractions. Offtime, for example, is an app that you can use to manage how much time you spend on your social media accounts, and even on texting. It also tracks how much time you use your devices, which can be a huge wake-up call! When you block the lure of the internet, and show yourself some tough-love discipline in this area, I think you'll be amazed at how much more efficient you will become with your precious time.

Basil Essential Oil will help you with setting boundaries! Basil is said to clear the heart and mind, and gives you the energy you need to deal with difficult people. Basil has long been used as a symbol of love and protection in Italy. Diffuse 2-3 drops of Basil alone, or with 2 drops of Lemon Essential Oil to help you build up the courage you may need to honor your feelings.

ESSENTIAL TAKE CARE TIP

#75 Color Coded Closet

When New York-based personal organizer and author Meryl Starr was a guest on my TV show, she motivated my viewers and me with her philosophy that finding happiness should be a priority. She showed us that clearing clutter in our lives can help us in our pursuit of happiness. Her easy-to-use ideas for how to do this have been featured in dozens of magazines.

One of these ideas was the focus of our segment together: closet organization. Starr says after you go through your closet and you decide what things you want to keep, organize them by color, rather than type. So, instead of hanging all of the skirts together, hang all of the blue things together (whether that's a skirt, jacket or a pair of pants).

Starr says that opening up our closets to that rainbow of color is uplifting, and also extremely functional. We tend to look for outfits by color anyway, she said, so just work with that. It will be easier for you to see what you have and find what you want.

Enjoy a fresh scent to go along with your clean closet with this easy-to-make air freshener:

ESSENTIAL AIR FRESHENER

Ingredients

10 Essential Oils

1 cup rice

1 small Mason jar

Fabric square big enough to cover more than the top of the jar

Ribbon long enough to tie around the top of the jar

Method

Add the rice to the jar. Add the Essential Oils of your choice. Some people like a light Lavender scent, others like a more invigorating, clean scent from a pine-based oil like Douglas Fir. You can have fun discovering your favorite scents. Center the fabric square on top of the jar and secure it by tying the ribbon around the rim. Place the jar on a closet shelf, and shake as needed to revitalize the scent. When the scent wears off (in about 3-4 months) you can add more Oils. These make great little gifts, too!

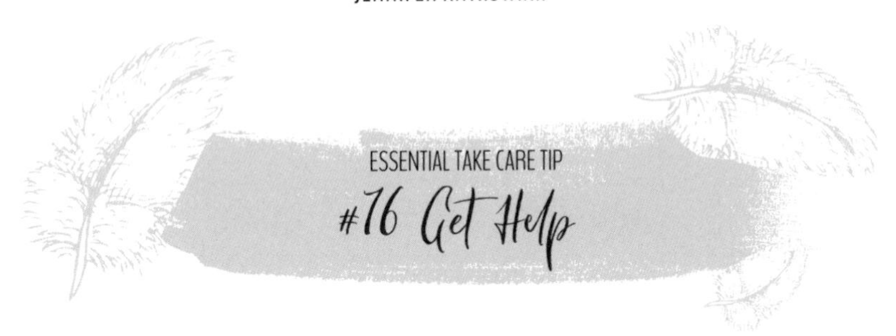

ESSENTIAL TAKE CARE TIP

#76 Get Help

If you're feeling overwhelmed because you're reading this chapter thinking, "I have more than a few extra pieces of paper hanging around!" there's help for you, too. If you have big bulky items you need to get rid of – worn furniture, for example – spend ten minutes Googling "junk removal" in your area. There are a bunch of national and local companies that specialize in big-time clutter clearing.

Most charge by the volume of the job (not the time it takes) and will provide a free evaluation and estimate of how much taking everything away will cost. If you decide to work with them, they'll schedule a time to come in a big truck (much less embarrassing than a bulldozer, and move everything out. It's fast, and all loading and cleanup is usually included in the price. Many companies make an effort to donate or recycle the items that you no longer need or want.

Another option is to find companies in your area that will help you to sell your unwanted items online. They'll photograph your things, list them online, and arrange for delivery. Though they'll charge a commission for each sale, but you'll get to clear out your space and make a little bit of extra money in the process.

We feel overwhelmed when we're stressed and afraid of the things that life is bringing us---that big feeling of waaaaaayyyy too much to do, and nowhere near enough time to do it. The tension associated with those feelings can make our muscles ache, our stomach sick, and our brain tired. A study done in 2008 to evaluate the impact of Essential Oils in nurses with high stress levels found that more than 57% of Intensive Care Unit nurses reported a decrease in perceived stress levels after using a combination of Lavender and Clary Sage Essential Oils. You can experience this for yourself by diffusing 2 drops of each, or by adding 8-10 drops of each to a 10ml rollerball bottle, filling it the rest of the way with Fractionated Coconut oil, then rolling it on your wrists, neck, and even over the heart.

ESSENTIAL TAKE CARE TIP

#77 Making Storage Work For You

Is it a metal bucket, or is it an art supply caddy? Is it an under-the-bed rolling storage box, or is it a game and puzzle cart that can be kept under the couch in the family room? It is what you make it! Think outside of the box, and customize your storage easily and inexpensively by re-purposing everyday items.

In selecting an efficient container, expert organizers say to look for something that:

- is sized to take up all the available space in the storage area so that you can maximize that prime piece of real estate. To fill a large space, use multiple stackable containers with lids.
- is see-through or allows you to clearly label it for fast finding.
- is sturdy enough to handle being bumped around and moved in and out as needed.

BONUS TIP: Remember to go through your storage containers for things that you don't regularly use at least once a year to make sure you still need everything that's in there. If you don't, let it go!

When I need to look at things in a different way, I reach for my Lemon Essential Oil. It's a cleansing Oil that helps to clear emotional clutter as well, and leave us feeling uplifted, and refreshed. Diffuse three drops of Lemon, or breathe it in straight from the bottle to help open your mind to new possibilities!

ESSENTIAL TAKE CARE TIP

#18 Organize your Oils

As you're reading this book and becoming more interested in using Essential Oils to support your physical and emotional health, you're probably starting to keep a little shopping list. I'm excited for you to either get started with Essential Oils, or...re-connect with them! Your collection will expand as you learn more about the benefits of each one, and in this chapter on Organization, I thought it would be great to give you some ideas on how to store your Oils in a way that makes it easy for you and your family to use and appreciate them.

You've got some decisions to make! What makes the most sense to you? Would it be easiest for you to find them alphabetically? By the benefits they provide? By the color on the bottle? I like to organize my main collection in wooden storage boxes alphabetically, but then I store duplicates in the room where I use them. For example, I keep Lavender on my nightstand to use for relaxation at bedtime, as well as Wild Orange and Peppermint to use for happy energy in the morning. I also keep a respiratory blend, and an immune support blend in rollerball bottles there so I have them readily accessible as part of my routines.

You can also use the time you're organizing your Oils to learn more about them. Are there any that you bought but never opened? Now's a great time to find out more about that Oil and start using it! It's also a good opportunity to take stock of your inventory, and make a note of any Oils you need to order, as well as things you want to add to your wish list. I've got some great Essential Oil information for you at www.TakeCareTips.com.

Get an energy boost for organizing with this diffuser blend:

TAKE CARE OF BUSINESS DIFFUSER BLEND

Ingredients		Method
2	Peppermint Essential Oil	Following the manufacturer's instructions that came with your diffuser, fill your diffuser with water, then add the drops of Oils.
1	Lemongrass Essential Oil	
1	Bergamot Essential Oil	

ESSENTIAL TAKE CARE TIP

#79 Live In The Moment

Even if you could fit into the size-6 bridesmaid's dress you wore to your sister's wedding, would you want to? Of course not. Then why is it still taking up space in your closet? If "because it makes me happy to think of how much skinnier I was then, and of all the fun our family had together on that day" is the reason, well, it's time to donate it.

One of the harshest clutter-clearing gurus on the decorating shows I watch likes to remind people that things are not memories. Getting rid of the bridesmaid's dress won't stop you from thinking of that happy day – no matter how spectacularly poofy the sleeves are.

Keep the memories, but get rid of much of the stuff you have from the past, and you'll make room to live happily in the here and now. Sometimes it helps to have a friend come by to give you a little tough love during this kind of cleaning process. If you can't bear to part with that purple dress with the huge shoulder pads, just because it was so expensive way back when, trust your friend when she directs it to the give-away pile.

BONUS TIP: If it's especially tough for you to part with certain items, you could take pictures of them to keep in a little scrapbook, or in an online folder, which would take up much less storage space.

If you're struggling with letting things go, it may be because you're not fully connected with living in (and loving) the present moment. An Essential Oil called Vetiver is known for its powerful ability to help with mindfulness, and support feelings of being comfortable where you are in life. It has an earthy scent that you may not appreciate at first sniff. No worries---to take the edge off, diffuse with a citrus Oil to brighten things up.

LIVE IN THE MOMENT DIFFUSER BLEND

Ingredients		Method
4	Wild Orange Essential Oil	Follow the directions that come with your diffuser to fill it with water, add your Oils, and enjoy.
2	Vetiver Essential Oil	
1	Rosemary Essential Oil	

ESSENTIAL TAKE CARE TIP

#80 Manage Your Mail

Paper clutter is a monster, isn't it? It seems to multiply while we sleep! Professional organizers say the best way to tame the paper beast once and for all is to set up a system for how you receive your mail. Block out the best time of your day to devote 10 minutes to going through it start to finish. Don't even touch it unless you have the time to sort everything that's there. Starting and stopping will only contribute to that pile of "unmade decisions".

Then, create a routine: first, pull out any obvious junk mail, and set it aside. Are you getting things you don't want? Keep only the contact information as a To Do item for later (you'll contact the company and tell them you want off their mail list). Place any bills in a priority pile of their own-you'll open them first. And finally, place personal correspondence (invitations, membership offers, etc.) in another stack.

As you're going through your bills, make note of information that is printed on the page about how to set up online payments – doing so will eliminate those pieces of paper coming to your house.

Enter any invitation information into your calendar, RSVP, and add the paper invitation to your recycling pile. If catalogs are an issue, visit www.catalogchoice.org where you can sign up to stop those unwanted catalogs and other junk mail from coming your way.

Many people like to go through their mail after work. Use your Oils to help create a smooth transition home. The Wild Orange brings happy energy, the Lavender calms, and the Rosemary allows you to keep some focus.

TRANSITION DIFFUSER BLEND

Ingredients		Method
3	Wild Orange Essential Oil	Follow the directions that come with your diffuser to fill it with water, add your Oils, and enjoy.
2	Lavender Essential Oil	
1	Rosemary Essential Oil	

ESSENTIAL TAKE CARE TIP

#81 Keep It Clean

When your home is organized, keeping it clean will be easier than ever before because everything will have a place. Once you've decided on some systems, I recommend a 10 minute clean-up at the end of every day, or every other day, with everyone helping out. This is really all it should take to stay on top of the clutter.

Keep your home smelling clean all the time with a room spray that you can customize in endless ways.

ESSENTIAL ROOM SPRAY

Ingredients

- 8 Eucalyptus Essential Oil
- 1 Lemon Essential Oil
- 8 oz. glass spray bottle
- Water
- 2 Tbsps. Witch Hazel, or Rubbing Alcohol (optional - see instructions)

Method

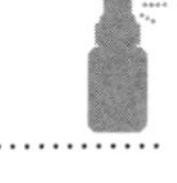

Add the water, Witch Hazel, or Rubbing Alcohol (if you like), along with the Essential Oils to the glass spray bottle. Witch Hazel and Rubbing Alcohol are natural emulsifiers, and help to keep the Oils mixed throughout the solution. As mentioned in earlier tips, Witch Hazel comes from leaves and twigs of a shrub and is used in a variety of personal care products for its benefits to the skin. Rubbing Alcohol (95% ethanol is recommended, which is easily available online or at hardware stores) acts as preservative, which will lengthen the life of your spray for a few months. You may choose to make this spray with just water but use or replace within a couple of weeks if not using Witch Hazel or Rubbing Alcohol. Shake and spritz around the room for instant freshening.

BONUS TIPS

To make sure you don't start to feel overwhelmed by all that stuff again, here are a few things to keep in mind as you go about your day:

- Analyze your shopping habits and make changes if necessary. Don't shop just to shop; always go out with a mission and a list.
- Don't buy something just because it's on sale. Nothing's a good deal if you didn't really want it to begin with.
- For every new item that you bring in, try to let something else go. If those shoes absolutely have your name on them, well then, there must be some old pair of sneakers in your closet that doesn't make you swoon so much anymore.

Each of these ideas reminds us to choose the things we have thoughtfully, with the goal of creating a productive and happy space in which to thrive.

Enjoy your favorite things every day by only owning your favorite things.

The American Journal of Nursing says strengthening personal and social relationships is a key benefit of caregiving. We often focus on the negative fallout from being a caregiver, but studies also show that caregivers are often happier, healthier, and live as much as five years longer.

CHAPTER
EIGHT

Why Don't You Do Something?

The title of this chapter is taken from a great piece of Mom Psychology. When you were growing up, your mom never liked to see you just sitting around, right? "Why don't you do something?" she'd probably say. Once again, mom was on to something: Just sitting around isn't good for us. Results of thirteen different studies on activity levels found that sitting for more than eight hours a day with no exercise carried a risk of dying similar to the risks of dying linked to obesity and smoking. Our brains need creative stimulation. Our bodies need physical stimulation.

It sounds paradoxical, but when we're busy and stressed out it's even more important to make time to do an activity just for the fun of it. Hobbies add color and excitement to life. I think one of the biggest challenges for many of us is to figure out how we can enjoy our own life while fulfilling our responsibilities to others. We might feel a little guilty even thinking about doing something light and free and fun. But I encourage you to give yourself permission to have fun, because lots of new research is showing that hobbies and other pleasant diversions are actually therapeutic!

Allowing yourself just a little break from financial worries, relationship issues and work pressures can be a wonderful thing. Don't worry – it'll all be there when you get back (sorry to say). Chances are, though, you'll be able to deal with all of it more efficiently after spending some time in a totally different, made-just-for-you world.

WHAT'S SO GREAT ABOUT HOBBIES?

It's simple: hobbies can bring happiness and joy to your life, and I want that for you. A few minutes with a hobby is an instant getaway from the tension and pressure of daily living. Doesn't that sound nice? Passive hobbies, like reading or listening to music, can bring pure mental and physical relaxation – and I'm all for that. But in this chapter I will focus on the more active, hands-on hobbies, like painting, beading or knitting. These will have those same calming benefits, but will also give you an added feeling of accomplishment, satisfaction and pride as you put the final touches on your project or master a new skill.

There's a sense of wholeness and balance that comes with hobbies. Because you've taken time to get in touch with and express your creative side (whether it's making something yourself or losing yourself in a book or a song), you are nurturing your many dimensions, and giving yourself room to be a well-rounded person. Those kinds of feelings carry over into other parts of your life. You'll have more confidence and perform better at work and at home.

I would like you to adopt a hobby. I included this chapter in the book because I want to help you get back to you, and a hobby is a small way to do that. I'm going to lean on you a little bit to think hard about what YOU like to do. Some caregivers I've talked with don't even know. A small part of who they are slips away every day, to the point that when you ask them what they like to do, they can only laugh a little and say, "Oh it's been a while since I've done anything. I just don't know."

That's so sad. You work hard to make things comfortable and happy for others - so let me ask: Is it OK to become so wrapped up in someone else's life that you lose the ability to find joy in your own? I didn't think so.

WHAT WOULD I EVEN DO?

C'mon, there's gotta be something you like to do. Maybe it's something you used to do when you were a child. Maybe it's something you've always wanted to do, but never took the time to try. Well, now's your chance. It's not too late. You can take piano or dance lessons whether you're 5 or 45 (or 85). I checked, and there's no law against it.

And guess what? I don't care, and neither should you, if you're good or bad at whatever it is that you enjoy doing! That's important. The great thing about being a grown up is that you get to be silly, exuberant, or even a little weird, and it's nobody's business if you are. A hobby is all about you, whether you're a latent Picasso or positively color-blind. You don't have to share your work with anyone, not even me (with the five kids, I don't have any more room on my refrigerator anyway). You're not doing this for a grade. I'll say it again: It's all about you. The only thing that matters is that you do it – whatever IT is.

As you work on your hobby, you'll notice that positive feelings start to flow. The passion you feel for what you're doing will help to generate happier, more productive attitudes about things in general. Once you find and ignite that passion, you can feel secure knowing that it's there for you whenever you need it. Soon you'll find that spending just a few minutes on your hobby can lower your stress level dramatically.

HEALTH BONUSES

A Swedish study, as well as research published in The New England Journal of Medicine, found that people who regularly spend even a little bit of time on hobbies that keep their brains active – things like sewing, gardening, or doing puzzles – are two-and-a-half times less likely to get Alzheimer's disease or other forms of dementia. A Japanese study of 12,000 people found that social hobbies can even boost immunity! It's also been shown that men with hobbies were less likely to die of stroke or circulatory disorders than those who did not have hobbies.

Certain types of hobbies have special benefits as well: knitting, crocheting, or anything that has you doing the same kinds of motions over and over, trigger that relaxation response we talked about in Chapter 2. This brings a feeling of peace, calm, and control. Your breathing actually slows down and your blood pressure lowers. Many studies have been done on hobbies as methods of stress-relief, and the findings are that yes, there is a distinct connection. Some psychologists think that hobbies can even pull people out of deep anxiety disorders. Hobbies let us move beyond our worries; they allow us to temporarily transcend our doubts and fears by giving us a glimpse of our own potential.

There are proven therapeutic benefits of hobbies for the estimated 70 million people in the U.S. who have some form of arthritis. Activities like knitting, crocheting, and gardening help with range of motion, and can significantly improve quality of life. Researchers at the University of Kansas found a lot of improvement in dexterity and hand and finger strength in patients with osteoarthritis who played the piano for twenty minutes, four times a week. An interesting note: Studies also show that people with arthritis are more likely to experience depression, and we know that caregivers are also at risk for developing depression. This is an example of how interlinked the issues affecting caregivers are … as well as the remedies.

GO WITH THE FLOW

Psychologists also talk about the medical benefits of achieving something they refer to as Flow, which represents the idea that there are certain activities in life that allow you to lose yourself in the moment. When you achieve Flow, your body and brain are in a state of stress-free, positive, flowing energy.

Studies show that hobbies can lead to Flow. For example, when you're playing a board game, the rules, objectives and goals are crystal clear. You can lose yourself in it. There's no need to think about what or how you need to do something. What a big difference from normal, daily life! You roll the dice and move your playing piece. That's it. While you're playing the game, your brain is free to relax because it's not being called upon to sort through any intense issue. It's all pretty cut and dried: just roll the dice and move your piece.

WHAT ELSE CAN HOBBIES DO FOR ME?

Hobbies can develop your creativity. They will help you stay more focused. The concentration you achieve through your hobby will help to awaken your mind and boost your energy levels.

You'll walk through life a little bit differently, as a multi-faceted person, with more motivation. Yes, you are a caregiver, but having a hobby shows you also respect and develop your own unique, special talents, from yo-yo tricks to creative writing. Fostering that feeling of self-worth through an interest in a hobby will help bring you a new interest in life in general.

Many life coaches and corporate motivators talk about the power of taking a break from routine. Doing that helps you to develop new, different ways of thinking, which can help on the job with better presentations, faster problem solving, and more productive relationships with colleagues and clients.

Hobbies also make it easier for you to connect with others. There are quilting groups, photography groups, flower arranging groups, and so many more. If you find the time, you might be able to go out and practice your hobby – and meet new friends – in a local group of fellow enthusiasts. Even the most obscure hobbies have online community forums where you can talk to lots of people who like some of the same things you do, from all over the world.

As you think about what you might like to do, don't get too fixated on the idea that you wouldn't know where to begin. Most craft enthusiasts are eager to help an interested newcomer get started. You'll find that most of these hobby groups welcome "newbies" and will be happy to share tips, encouragement and interesting conversation along the way.

COOL HOBBY FACTS

Some wonderful discoveries have come out of simple hobbies. For example, medical researcher Alexander Fleming discovered Penicillin by accident when he noticed an unusual mold growing on some of the Petri dishes that he left out while he was experimenting with different cultures – this was his hobby, which eventually became his profession.

There may also be a connection between extremely smart and productive people, and hobbies. A professor at Michigan State University found that among more than 100 Nobel Prize winners in the field of Chemistry, nearly all had a hobby of some kind, and more than half had at least one artistic hobby.

SOUNDS GOOD, BUT HOW CAN I POSSIBLY MAKE TIME FOR A HOBBY?

Remember what I've told you about the health benefits of hobbies, and try to think about a hobby as a necessity. Tell yourself, "this is not a fun break from reality; this is an important exercise that I simply must do to help me to be better at my other work." That may help to get rid of any guilty feelings you have about the time-for-yourself issue.

You can make spending time on your hobby feel like a priority by actually scheduling it in your planner. But don't get bogged down trying to find time that you can block out. Any little bit will do to get you started. It doesn't have to be smack dab in the middle of your busy day.

For example, one of the things I used to like to do was make scrapbooks. I found that the best time for me to do that was at night, after the kids were in bed. It was a very quiet, peaceful time in this normally busy house. I had some tea, I would sit and look through family pictures, and that always brought a smile to my face, no matter what happened all the other hours of my day. It's so nice to end the day with a hobby that lets you go to bed feeling relaxed and happy.

If you need more structure, or more of a push to get you to try something, you could take 10 minutes to find a class in your area. If you register and pay, you might feel more obligated to go and spend that time on yourself!

There are many ways that you can get the benefits of the hobby of your choice in small chunks of time throughout the day. Just find a way to get started. I'm hoping that you'll like your new hobby so much, you'll end up spending more than 10 minutes every few days enjoying it. Here then are just some of the many stress-relieving hobbies perfectly suited for caregivers, and busy people in general:

ESSENTIAL TAKE CARE TIP

#82 Gardening

Some of my earliest memories are of my parents and me in the big garden behind our house. I was a little girl who never really minded dirt or worms, and I still don't. Gardening gets you out to feel the warm sunshine and soak up some Vitamin D. It lets your lungs take in some fabulous fresh air. It gets you wonderfully covered in mud, if you're doing it with gusto. And growing beautiful plants from tiny seeds or cuttings gives you a huge sense of accomplishment.

Some of my most relaxing moments in the garden don't even involve the pretty part of the hobby. I find peace in just a few minutes of weeding or raking. It's active work that still allows you to daydream, and it feels great to see everything looking so nice when you're done.

There's science behind these happy feelings. There's a whole profession called Horticultural Therapy that is based on the spirit-soothing powers of working with plants. Horticultural therapists work to relieve stress among nursing home patients, the physically challenged, and prisoners. The artist Claude Monet used his garden to pull himself out of a deep depression. He then made paintings of it in the hopes of helping others to heal.

world. There is a lot of hope in that. If you sometimes struggle to see the beauty around you, the camera can help you get back in touch with the color and light in your own world. You might find that you share that struggle with your loved one. Open their eyes through what yours are able to capture.

You can have fun setting up different themes for your photo shoots if you like. As you practice seeing and capturing life through a lens, you will begin to see things differently. Even a simple digital camera (where you can just delete the bad pictures…) can get you started, with no great skill required. But feel free to go as fancy or in-depth as you want. Keep a camera in your purse, pocket or glove compartment, so you can grab it and go if you're out and about with an extra ten minutes on your hands. It's as simple as aiming, then clicking the shutter.

Enhance feelings of gratitude for the beauty around you with this roller ball blend:

I AM GRATEFUL BLEND

Ingredients

- 4 Bergamot Essential Oil
- 3 Wild Orange Essential Oil
- 2 Frankincense Essential Oil
- 2 Geranium Essential Oil
- 10 ml Rollerball Bottle
- Fractionated Coconut Oil

Method

Add all Essential Oils to a 10 ml roller bottle. Add Fractionated Coconut Oil to fill to the top. Apply to pulse points.

This blend contains a citrus Oil. It is advised, due to photosensitivity, not to expose the area of the skin that citrus Oils have been applied to, for at least 12 hours after application.

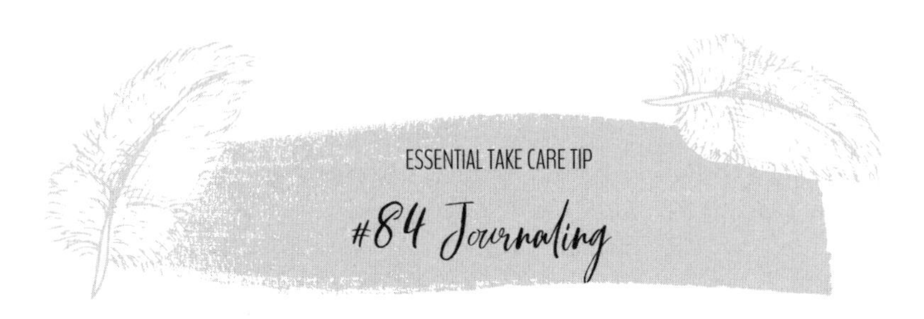

ESSENTIAL TAKE CARE TIP

#84 Journaling

Exploring and writing down your own thoughts is a wonderful way to express things that you might feel, but are never able to say. Writing can help stimulate new ideas or calm your fears.

Journaling is an easy hobby to fit into your day. Keep a notebook handy so that when you find yourself sitting at a doctor's office, waiting to pick someone up from school, or by the side of a loved one who's resting or sleeping, you can jot down a few thoughts. If you're at the computer all day, consider taking 10 minutes when you're done with your regular work to type any thoughts that have been swirling around your head. This is just for you – a nice way to end your workday.

It's also a perfect hobby you can share with the person you're caring for. This was one of the things that kept me going while I was caring for my mother-in-law, Me-ma, after her cancer diagnosis.

Her favorite color was blue. I bought a blue leather journal and we called it "her book." Late at night when I'd go back to her house after the late newscast, we'd sit together and I'd write. She told me so many interesting stories about her childhood and growing up with her brother and sister in an orphanage.

I asked her about her husband and about each one of her children and grandchildren. What things she loved about each of them. What she hoped for each of them. Special times that she remembered sharing with each of them.

This hobby was for both of us. It was a way for her to share stories and feelings that she didn't want to be forgotten. It offered me a sense of control. Here was something concrete and positive that I could bring to the situation to make it a little bit better.

I left Me-ma's house the rainy night that she died, came home, and typed long excerpts from that little blue leather book into my computer. I sent them to 24-hour copy center and asked them to print me a dozen bound books.

I was able to give them to our family after the funeral mass. It was extremely rewarding to be able to offer something positive at that time…something that would help keep her spirit close.

You see, hobbies aren't just ways to pass the time, but tools for the spirit. You may want to try sharing a journal with someone, like I did, or you can just keep it to yourself. It is truly up to you to decide where your hobby belongs in your life.

Another great time to journal is before bed. Take just a couple of minutes to jot down five things you're grateful for from the day. You'll be able to fall asleep with those happy, uplifting thoughts in mind. It will also help you to recognize and appreciate the good things in your life, which can be humbling. What a beautiful part of a bedtime routine!

Frankincense or Rose Essential Oils are both wonderful choices to support journaling. Both help to calm the mind, and support the brain. In fact, many use these Oils with meditation. That peaceful feeling will make it easier for you to connect with thoughts you want to express. Diffuse a few drops of either of these Oils, or add a drop to a few drops of Fractionated Coconut Oil and apply to your wrists and the back of your neck. Lemon is a much less expensive alternative, and the citrus Oils are great to help clear and open your mind.

ESSENTIAL TAKE CARE TIP

#85 Puzzles

Seems like the only time my family thinks to break out a puzzle is when we stumble across a few tucked in a closet some place we're staying on vacation. We find a space to set it up and it stays there until it's done. Sometimes it takes us all week to finish a big puzzle with lots of little pieces, but we chip away at it just a little bit at a time, and it all comes together. Sometimes just one of us works on it; another time, we work on it together.

Working on puzzles is a nice hobby because it's inexpensive. It's also very quiet, so you can do it early in the morning or late at night, while people are sleeping.

Puzzles were part of that study I told you about earlier– one of the active-mind activities that will help to prevent all kinds of dementia. If you're feeling especially hungry for a brain challenge, find one of those intentionally difficult puzzles and have at it!

Does your brain need a boost? Ancient Greeks and Romans believed Rosemary helped with memory. Recent research shows students who breathed in Rosemary Oil before a test had higher scores! Clary Sage is known for its calming properties. Lemon Essential Oil acts as a cleanser---we use it in cleaning solutions for our homes, but it's a powerful cleanser for our brains, too! Encourage mental sharpness with this diffuser blend:

SHARP THINKING DIFFUSER BLEND

Ingredients		Method
3	Rosemary Essential Oil	Follow the directions that come with your diffuser to fill it with water, add your Oils, and enjoy.
2	Clary Sage Essential Oil	
2	Lemon Essential Oil	

ESSENTIAL TAKE CARE TIP

#86 Scrapbooking

While journaling allows you to tell a story through words, scrapbooking lets you tell it through pictures. You can tap into a lot of creative energy by working with your hands to clip, design and embellish.

Although I've seen (and made) very ornate scrapbooks, I know that it's easy to get lost or intimidated in the scrapbooking aisle. But really, you just need a few basic supplies to get started:

- Some photos
- A blank Scrapbook
- A pair of scissors (to cut photos or paper as needed)
- Some acid-free paper (It's treated so it won't damage your photos. You can find it anywhere you buy craft supplies)
- An acid-free pen or thin marker (so that you can add a little bit of journaling or captions. These are sold in craft, office supply and photo stores)
- An acid-free glue stick or adhesive squares for attaching your photos to the pages (you'll find it right with the scrapbooking stuff)

You can do a lot in ten-minute chunks to advance your scrapbooking hobby: You can organize and select photos you'd like to use on a page. You can write some notes to go with the photos, or your journaling thoughts. You can go through your stash and choose what papers you'd like to use.

Then, when you have a little more time, you can have fun bringing all of the elements together to create a page. It's pretty hard to get bored with scrapbooking. There are always new products and techniques to try.

Now, as I said before, your hobby is yours; your scrapbook can be your own private collection of memories, or if you like, a gift for the family and a keepsake for all to enjoy.

If you like the idea of scrapbooking, but aren't excited by the idea of gathering up and storing scrapbooking supplies, there are many digital scrapbooking tools that help you organize and highlight your memories. It's not quite the same as feeling the elements in your hands, but it will provide the same kind of creative fuel for your brain.

Tap into aromatherapy to stimulate your creative juices---it's believed Leonardo Da Vinci did! His favorite creativity-boosting scent is thought to be Neroli! Neroli Essential Oil comes from the flower of the bitter orange tree. The scent brightens the mood, and helps to reduce any anxious feelings. Diffuse a few drops of Neroli, or mix a drop with a few drops of Fractionated Coconut Oil and apply it to your wrists, behind the ears, and over the heart.

ESSENTIAL TAKE CARE TIP

#87 Knitting, Crocheting & Needlework

Needle arts go back thousands of years, and just recently there's been a big resurgence in knitting, crocheting and other types of needlework. People who know and love this hobby have raved about its health benefits for a long time, and now, people in the medical community are starting to agree.

The mind-calming, strengthening and balancing effects of knitting are said to be similar to the kinds of feelings you can achieve through yoga. A Harvard Medical School Mind/Body Institute report shows that when a person knits, their heart rate and blood pressure drop. Several organizations are paying attention to these findings and are now offering knitting classes and groups in cancer support centers, hospices, corporate health and wellness programs, senior citizen's centers and even children's hospitals.

Learning the basics of knitting doesn't take a lot of time. And if you need some help, many craft stores offer low-cost classes. People who go say they love the little communities created there. You can also search YouTube for easy tutorials.

To soothe your hands and wrists after repetitive work like this, you can use pre-made Essential Oil infused therapeutic rubs, or make your own. The Oils in this blend all work to soothe and invigorate tired muscles and joints. They are anti-inflammatory, as well.

SOOTHING HAND CREAM

Ingredients

- 5 Peppermint Essential Oil
- 5 Eucalyptus Essential Oil
- 3 Copaiba Essential Oil
- 1/2 cup solid Coconut Oil

Method

In a small bowl, mix all the ingredients together. If you'd like a lighter consistency, use a hand mixer to whip the mixture. Store in a small glass jar. Massage into your hands and wrists as needed.

ESSENTIAL TAKE CARE TIP

#88 No-Sew Crafts

If it's been a while since you've tried any crafting, or if you don't consider yourself crafty at all, but you'd like to try something, I have two words for you: Polar Fleece.

Just looking at the rainbow of available polar fleece colors all lined up on the shelves of the fabric store will bring a smile to your face. Polar Fleece is soft and cuddly. It doesn't fray. It's criminally easy to work with.

Making a cozy scarf or a throw blanket is as simple as cutting a piece of polar fleece to the size you want. You can cut fringe around the edge to finish your project off.

You didn't skip over the rest of the directions. Cut and fringe. You're done! Visit me at www.TakeCareTips.com for some helpful videos for quick projects.

I like to make reversible throws by cutting out two pieces of fleece in different colors. Place the pieces together, and make a four-or-five-inch fringe all the way around, cutting through both pieces. Bring one piece of fringe in each color together and tie in a knot. Do that the whole way around.

These fast, easy, inexpensive projects make thoughtful gifts. Customize them by using your favorite team's colors (it's all Black and Gold here!), or school colors.

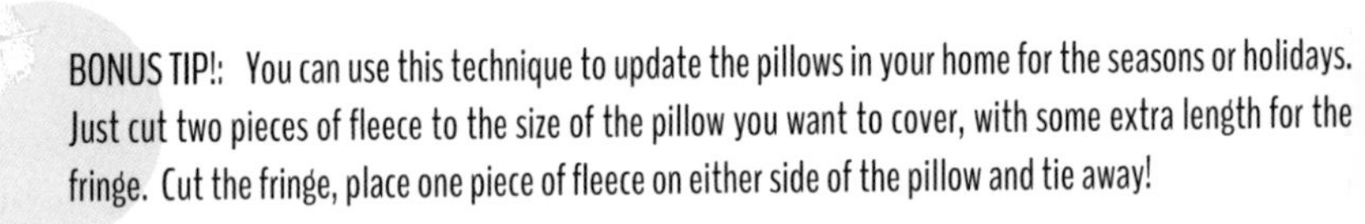

BONUS TIP!: You can use this technique to update the pillows in your home for the seasons or holidays. Just cut two pieces of fleece to the size of the pillow you want to cover, with some extra length for the fringe. Cut the fringe, place one piece of fleece on either side of the pillow and tie away!

While we're thinking warm and cozy thoughts…there are Essential Oils that have warming properties! Make sure to blend these with Fractionated Coconut Oil (or another carrier oil) to avoid any skin irritation. Massage this blend on your hands and feet to help you warm up!

WARMING MASSAGE BLEND

Ingredients

- 2 Cinnamon Bark Essential Oil
- 8 Lavender Essential Oil
- 4 Black Pepper Essential Oil
- Fractionated Coconut Oil
- 10 ml Rollerball Bottle

Method

Add the Essential Oils to the roller ball bottle. Fill to the top with fractionated coconut oil.

Remember to wash your hands after you massage with this blend, to avoid getting any in your eyes.

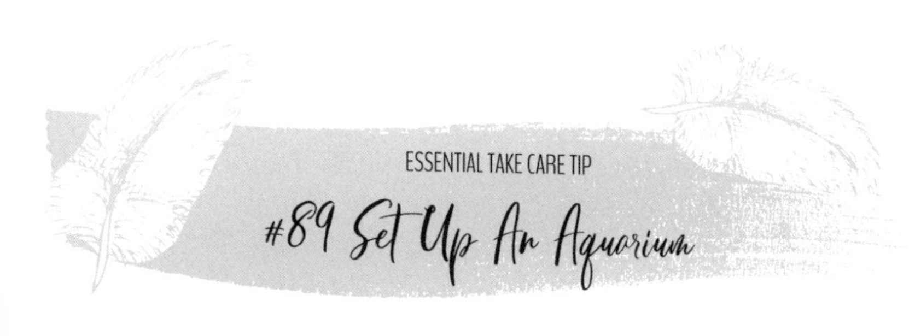

ESSENTIAL TAKE CARE TIP

#89 Set Up An Aquarium

It can be as little as a tiny bowl with some colored rocks and one little Beta fish, or something more extravagant with several varieties of tropical fish. Watching fish do their thing is another hobby that has been proven to reduce blood pressure and relieve stress.

No wonder then that I've noticed fish tanks filled with beautiful, mesmerizing fish in dentist waiting rooms, hospitals and hospices. Many corporate offices install fish tanks in their lobbies as well.

Keeping fish requires regular, but not really very time-consuming, care. And, another part of the fun of this hobby is learning about the fish you're keeping. Check out on-line resources and books at pet stores to find out more about the fascinating under sea world.

Bring a beachy feeling into your home anytime with this diffuser blend featuring bright, happy scents.

BEACH HOUSE DIFFUSER BLEND

Ingredients

- 2 Wild Orange Essential Oil
- 2 Sandalwood Essential Oil
- 2 Grapefruit Essential Oil

Method

Follow the directions that come with your diffuser to fill it with water, add your Oils, and enjoy.

Whether they're sparkly and shiny, or rough and earthy, beads are fun and relaxing to work with. Planning, placing and creating your bead project calls upon motor, visual and cognitive skills. If you're new to the art of beadwork, a very simple project is a lava bead Essential Oil Diffuser Bracelet. (I have videos for you on diffuser bracelets and more about the Oils I like to use in diffuser jewelry at www.TakeCareTips.com!)

DIFFUSER BRACELET

Materials

- Beads of your choice (check out the Resource Section at the end of this book for ideas on where to buy beads and complete DIY kits)
- Lava Beads (porous beads that act as mini diffusers)
- Stretch cording
- Scissors
- Craft Glue

Method

Measure the cording around your wrist and cut a piece, leaving a little extra room to be able to tie a knot. Tie a knot near the end of one side of the cording, and begin stringing beads in the design you'd like. Be sure to include at least one lava bead. Leave enough room at the end of the cording so that you can tie the two ends together. Apply a drop of glue over the knot to reinforce it, and when it's dry, slide a bead from the bracelet over the knot to hide it.

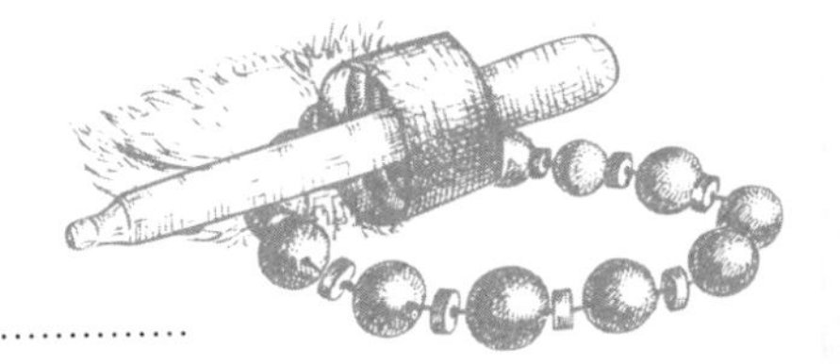

You've just created a way for you to take your aromatherapy on the go! Just add a drop of any favorite Essential Oil or Oil blend to the lava bead. It will keep the scent for a few days. You can refresh it as needed. Some of my favorite Oils to wear on my diffuser bracelets include Wild Orange, Magnolia, and Bergamot.

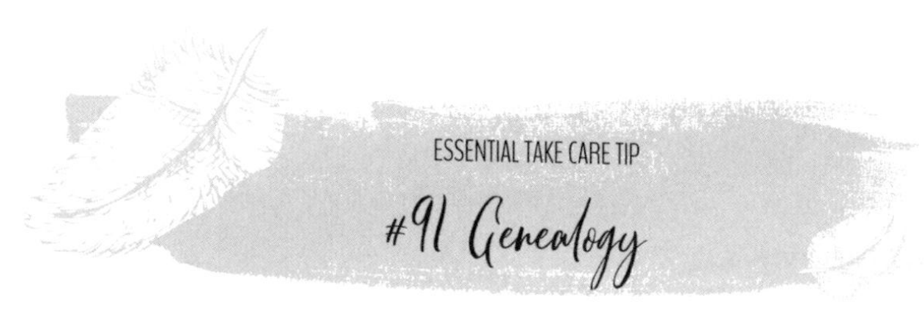

ESSENTIAL TAKE CARE TIP

#91 Genealogy

Have you ever spent some time getting to know your family history? Maybe you're related to a founding father, or royalty. Maybe your family suffered through poverty or slavery. Maybe you are related to an infamous criminal!

Genealogy involves searching for and then using a variety of archived records to trace your family connections. New technology has made it easier than ever to find old birth and death certificates, marriage licenses and property titles that can provide interesting clues for where you came from.

There are plenty of expensive family tree services out there ready to help you, but you don't need to get pulled into any of that. Chances are good you'll be able to get things rolling for free with a call to your city library. Many have people there who are able to help you find family records. You can gather up any names, dates, and family paperwork that you might already have to help with the process, and take them with you. But, really, with just your name, birth date, and the place you were born, the person at the library will be able to help you to find out quite a bit about your relatives. Also, websites like www.ellisisland.org and www.familysearch.org offer access to their archives for free.

Deciding to pursue genealogy makes you a family detective. You will be able to spend as little as a few minutes, or much longer, reviewing the information you gather. With each discovery, you'll get more information that will help your next search. You can keep chipping away with your own Internet searches. This is another one of those hobbies you can share. Think about interviewing older family members to help fill in some of the blanks.

Tracing your family heritage will be fun and exciting, and may even provide a sense of comfort and security as you connect to your own remarkable and deep roots.

We all crave being part of a family. It's natural for humans to want to connect, and fee a sense of togetherness. Cedarwood Essential Oil is known to support a deep feelin of community. Cedarwood trees have deep roots and grow very tall, which some sa connects them to heaven and earth. Diffuse a few drops of Cedarwood to feel a specia sense of belonging.

Family and friendships are two of the greatest facilitators of happiness.

–John C. Maxwell

Are you being realistic about your role as a caregiver? So much time is spent trying to control what we simply cannot control. Let those things go, and put the time and energy toward taking better care of yourself.

CHAPTER NINE

Let Me See A Smile

I've cared for people I loved (still love) who were dying. The process is consuming to the point that you can feel like part of you is dying, too. I fully understand that putting on a happy face when you're a caregiver, is not always possible. In this chapter, I'll tell you why you shouldn't force positive feelings, but I'll teach you how you can connect with them, and allow yourself to feel some comfort and peace.

As I write this book, I'm constantly thinking about all of the different kinds of caregivers who will read it:

- "Traditional" caregivers who are caring for a terminally ill loved one
- The "Sandwich Generation" caring for children AND parents who need support
- Those who have taken it upon themselves to take care of friends, neighbors, and co-workers

- Those who choose to be foster parents and adopters, providing a home and love to children whose biological parents aren't able to give them those things
- Single parents who struggle to keep everything together
- Professional caregivers – doctors, nurses, therapists, and other skilled providers who often care for patients and work, and then come home to take care of family members

Let yourself envision just a little portion of each of those journeys for a few minutes. Try to put yourself in that caregiver's shoes for a day. Imagine the extremely challenging, troubling, draining circumstances that would be part of their everyday life.

It's NORMAL for you to have low times, when the overwhelming nature of your world gets the better of you, and life feels heavy and dark. It's WRONG to think you must ignore or hide your feelings and put on a strong front for others. Covering them up doesn't make them go away. In fact, as we've learned throughout this book, failing to express and deal with our feelings leads to a variety of serious negative physical and emotional fallout.

BE HONEST WITH YOURSELF

I want to tell you about creating positive thoughts – which is not the same as "being happy all the time." I don't even know if it's possible to be happy all the time. Caring for someone you love brings out a big range of emotions.

I'd like to introduce you to Anthony Rapp. He's the Broadway star who originated the role of Mark Cohen in *Rent*. He's also a New York Times Best-Selling author of his book, *Without You: A Memoir of Love, Loss, and the Musical Rent*. It includes stories about his days in *Rent*, but also about his mother's long struggle with cancer.

Years ago, Rapp launched a stage version of *Without You* at the City Theatre in Pittsburgh. I was in the audience and was moved to tears by the heart-felt way he spoke and sang about his mother, and his relationship with her. After the show, I sought him out for an interview for this book, which he graciously agreed to.

Rapp was quick to point out that he was not the day-to-day caregiver for his mother. He was living and working in New York City, exactly where his mother told him she wanted him to be, during much of her illness, but he visited her, spent time with her, and was there to see some of her good days and some of the not-so-good ones.

"There were moments when I felt I lost my mind," Rapp told me. "My nerve endings seemed so exposed, so raw. But I learned something that I want to get across to others through my show: Be honest with yourself - with the anger or whatever you are feeling. That's part of taking care of you. Feeling the anger, the depression, the fear, the resistance; it's all part of it. Any feelings you resist, or deny, or ignore will come back to bite you. What you resist persists."

Through his experience with *Rent*, Rapp was introduced to Friends in Deed, a caregiver support group based in New York. He ended up serving on the organization's board of directors. Their mission is to help people, and their message is simple: we're all in the same boat. "At Friends," he said, "a person who just lost someone to AIDS could be sitting next to someone caring for someone with cancer. The people who need support are not broken up into categories; and it's set up that way on purpose, so that everyone understands that no one is alone. They may have different specifics involved with their situations, but they are all feeling the same range of emotions."

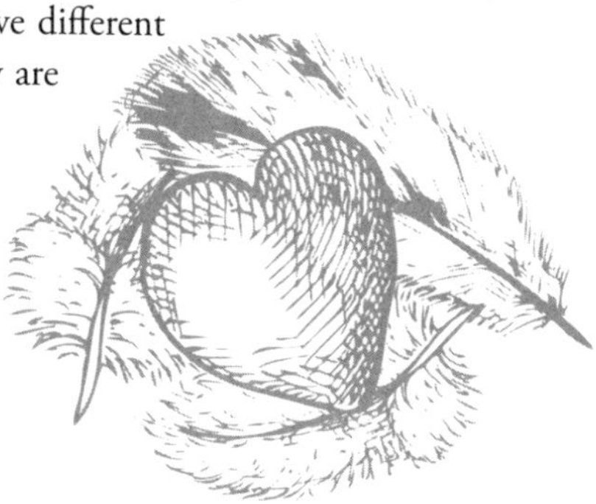

In this chapter you will see that you can be sad. You can be scared. You can be mad. AND, you can remain positive through it all. You have the power to retrain your brain and turn negative thinking into positive living. Are you open to that? Read on...

BUT THERE'S SO MUCH TO FEEL NEGATIVE ABOUT

Sure, there are plenty of days when it seems like it's easier to see the negative side of daily life. With health problems, big bills, too many things and not enough time swirling around you, it can be tough to find some good in all of it...something to smile about.

The search for something good can feel like a lot of work - one more thing to add to your already overwhelming list. So, you cave. You stop even trying to be positive. You let one little bad thing grow bigger and spoil your whole day. Soon, you find yourself grumbling your way from one day to the next – maybe dredging up a "happy face" for others, maybe not.

The wildly popular book, *The Secret,* put a spotlight on centuries-old concepts regarding the power of positive thinking. Very simply, it revolves around the idea that thoughts are magnets. So, one negative thought attracts more negative thoughts. Positive thoughts work the same way, but are said to be even stronger. If you ever took a physics class you learned that like attracts like. It's the same with our thoughts.

You have the power to decide what magnet you're going to pull out of that brain and use today. Are you fishing for negative thoughts and experiences, or do you want to try to pull in some positive ones? It's all up to you.

Getting your brain to change over to being more positive will take some time. You will probably have moments and days where you slip up. And that's OK as long as you accept that becoming more positive is a process, and that it can really work for you. A little bit every day, and you're there. Before long, thinking about things in a better way will start to just come naturally.

Remember, there are a whole lot of feel-good endorphins in your brain just waiting to be activated!

WHERE WILL POSITIVE THINKING GET ME?

Believing that you are capable of positive things will help you to achieve positive things. Positive thinking is a great motivator. Negative thoughts hold you back from realizing your full potential. Don't shortchange yourself.

What coach would be worth his salt if he told his team, "Well, the other team looks to be in better condition, and better skilled. They've won more games than we have this season, and I really don't see us being able to beat them. Don't get hurt out there!"

Ha! Can you imagine that happening? No! The coach is in there saying, "We have a challenge in front of us today and we are ready for this challenge. We have worked hard for this and now the opportunity is here for us to take it. Let's get out there and beat this team!"

Those are the kinds of winning attitudes that top business leaders and other successful people speak of. If it works for them, it can work for us. Choosing to have positive attitudes will help you to feel more confident in yourself, and in your abilities to do whatever it is you want to do.

The importance of these kinds of feelings and how to teach yourself to feel them is being studied in a newer branch of psychology called Positive Psychology, founded by Dr. Martin Seligman. His research indicates that people have the ability to train themselves to be happier, no matter how they were raised or what is involved in their current life situations.

However, there are doubters out there in the medical community regarding this positive thinking stuff. Can positive thinking directly cause you to be healthier? Some researchers argue that the issue is just too complex to be that clear cut.

Positive thinking can't hurt you in any way, though. It's not like trying some new experimental pill. So I say, why not try it, and see if you feel the benefits that so many others have?

GETTING STARTED: THE BASICS

When we have negative thoughts about something, we react in a negative way. So to get a different response, we need to think differently. Over the years, I have interviewed several psychologists regarding positive thinking techniques, and many have suggested that the fastest way to get the brain retraining process started comes down to this: you need to replace your negative thoughts with positive ones.

Easier said than done, you say? I agree. But... the first step in changing something is to recognize that it needs to be changed, and by buying this book, you've already shown you're there.

Mindset coaches teach us that as soon as you begin to feel a negative thought registering, quickly and actively stop everything and focus on replacing it with something positive. If you are imagining all of the worst things that could happen, deliberately and consciously tell yourself about all of the best things that will happen. Practice that kind of thinking every chance you get, and soon you'll notice it will start to happen on its own. Plus, the positive thoughts will trigger your brain to start firing up those delicious-feeling endorphins to support you along the way.

WHAT'S FAITH GOT TO DO WITH IT?

My own experiences have taught me that faith goes hand in hand with positive thinking. Research has shown that people who are tuned in spiritually have an easier time pulling through tough times.

I've seen that the caregiving journey presents many opportunities for us to find ourselves at a crossroads in our faith; where we seriously question why God (or the Creator or the Universe) would allow such pain.

- Are you mad that God would let your loved one suffer?
- Are you mad at God for putting this burden on you?
- Are you ashamed that you feel that way?

It's at this point that some people choose to turn away from God. However, I believe that clinging to your spiritual connection, especially if you are doubting its purpose in your life, becomes the light you need to pull yourself up and out of the darkness. Faith can fill in the hole you sometimes feel in your heart.

As I told you earlier, when I got the phone call that my mother had died, I got in the car to head home and be with my family, but I ended up making an un-planned pit stop at my church. It wasn't my intention to go there…I was just kind of drawn to it.

That quick visit to pray gave me the spiritual boost I needed to be in a more positive mindset as I continued home.

A WHITE FEATHER STORY

When things quieted down a bit after my mom's funeral, some angry feelings started to bubble up. I sat in my living room, closed my eyes and told God that I didn't understand why He needed my mom more than I did. Through tears of frustration and grief I told Him how much I missed her, and I demanded a sign that she would still be with me in some way.

A movie was on in the background, and right at that moment, I happened to glance up and saw an image of a big, fluffy, white feather floating across the TV screen.

I didn't sleep well that night and the next morning I woke up, still mad, and with a puffy face from crying. I stomped around getting ready for work…stomped out to my car still feeling confused, and abandoned by God…and I noticed something stuck in the driver's door.

It was a big, fluffy, white feather.

A warm feeling washed over me and took my breath away. I smiled, teared up, and was filled with gratitude. It was my sign.

I've been finding white feathers ever since. They seem to show up just when I am needing a hug from my mom. At one time or another each of my children has come running to me, smiling and waving a white feather saying, "it's from your mom!"

I share that story in my Take Care Tips talks, and it's very common for someone in the audience to approach me afterward with a similar experience; like the time a burly, but soft-spoken man shared that when he was growing up his father told him that pennies were an angel's way of saying hello. His father suffered an illness and died. Since then, the man has found shiny pennies in unexpected places, such as the dirty construction sites where he works. He told me his faith, and those pennies, are what help him cope with the loss of his dad.

The Rev. Daniel E. Hall, MD, is an Episcopal priest and assistant professor at the University of Pittsburgh. As the first ever Fellow of Religion and Medicine at Duke University, he conducted research on the associations between religion and health. He found that in terms of improved life span, the effect of regular attendance at religious services is about the same as that of regular physical exercise; according to him, both add approximately 3-5 years of life! Dr. Hall explains it this way:

"The data are still inconclusive, but there's growing evidence to suggest that the religious belief and practice of patients have a concrete, measurable impact on their health and healthcare. Prayer, worship and participation in religious communities not only "improves" health, but it also provides an important way patients weave the experience of illness into their lives in meaningful ways."

A religious leader in my church reminds me that giving yourself permission to feel mad at God can actually bring you closer to Him, and to positive thinking. I asked him what he would say to a caregiver who feels a lot of anger towards God. I was surprised at his answer. "Tell Him," he said, "Yell at Him. Scream that you're mad."

"Seriously?" I asked.

"Yes," he said. "God can take it."

How beautiful is that? Go ahead and unload. God can take it.

My faith teaches me that God loves you, no matter what.

With that to motivate us, let's get to some 10-minute tips for positive thinking.

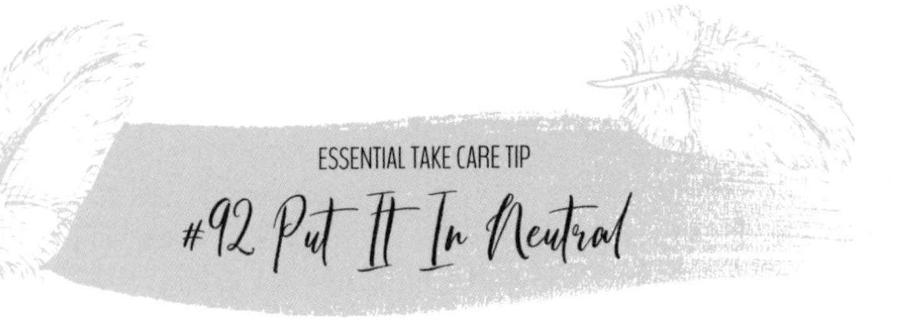

Before you go all in with trying to change negative thoughts to positive ones, try going to neutral. Nurses do this. They don't hit you with, "Are you in a lot of pain?"
It's usually more like, "Tell me how you're feeling." The idea behind this is that you shouldn't plant the seed for pain by saying the word "pain".

You can do this as you move through your own day, too. Instead of, "I hate having to wait this long at the doctor's office!" Try, "It's a little tough to be patient sometimes." See how that small change takes some of the heat away?

There's a proprietary blend of Essential Oils I use that was specifically created to help you move into neutral! It's known as the Grounding Blend. The Oils in it include Spruce Leaf, Ho Wood, Frankincense, Blue Tansy, Blue Chamomile, and Osmanthus. Any one of those individual Oils, or Lavender, Clary Sage, or Cedarwood can also help you feel centered. I like to apply a drop of the Grounding Blend to the bottom of each foot in the morning. It helps me feel like I'm ready to take on whatever the day brings, with a calm, controlled mind. I have more about the Oils I use and where you can get them at www.TakeCareTips.com.

ESSENTIAL TAKE CARE TIP

#93 Embrace Change

As a caregiver, your world can feel like it's changing at a very fast pace. When I was caring for my mother-in-law, and her health was declining, I remember feeling like I never had time to fully digest any one part, before something else would change. That's a really stressful cycle.

Change will happen. We can't avoid it, but we do have a choice as to how we react to it. A positive mindset will allow us to more readily embrace change as an opportunity for growth, instead of fearing it.

I took comfort in learning that dealing with change is a process. Psychologists have identified six steps for change that take you through the whole path from the first thought of change, through the action, and then letting it become part of your new way of life.

The emotional benefits of Essential Oils can help you keep a positive outlook as you deal with the changes in your life. Here's a blend you can make with Oils that will give you a feeling of confidence and support.:

I'VE GOT THIS DIFFUSER BLEND

Ingredients

2 **Cedarwood Essential Oil**
supports you to hold steady and hang in there

2 **Lime Essential Oil**
cleanses feelings of sadness, or grief, and gives a feeling of happy energy

1 **Rosemary Essential Oil**
helps the mind to focus during challenges

Method

Following the manufacturer's instructions for your diffuser, fill it with water, add the Oils, and diffuse to create a positive environment.

ESSENTIAL TAKE CARE TIP

#94 Be Grateful

There has been much talk about the benefits of having "an attitude of gratitude." By being thankful for all of the big and little things in your life, you are opening your heart and mind to allow even more good things to come on in.

If you're having a hard time finding something to be thankful for, you can have some fun while getting your brain to respond the way you want it to. Find a part of your body that you're not having any trouble with, and take a few moments to focus on the joy of that. Let yourself get over-the-top, inappropriately happy about it. How's your little finger doing? Is the nail attached? Does it bend where it's supposed to? WOW! You have an awesome little finger! Isn't that great? Nothing wrong there!

As silly as that sounds, psychologists say your brain will pick up on those positive thoughts, and as we've discussed, soon these positive thoughts will come more easily.

I can't remember where I read this quote, but I've always loved it:

> *"Gratitude and negativity cannot co-exist."*

Make this rollerball blend to support feelings of gratitude:

I FEEL GRATEFUL ROLLERBALL BLEND

Ingredients

8	Bergamot Essential Oil
6	Copaiba Essential Oil
6	Sandalwood Essential Oil

Fractionated Coconut Oil

10 ml Rollerball Bottle

Method

Add all Essential Oils to a rollerball bottle. Add Fractionated Coconut Oil to fill to the top. Replace the rollerball and apply to pulse points. Bergamot is from the citrus family, and remember, Citrus Oils are phototoxic.

It is advised, due to photosensitivity, not to expose the area of the skin that citrus Oils have been applied to, for at least 12 hours after application.

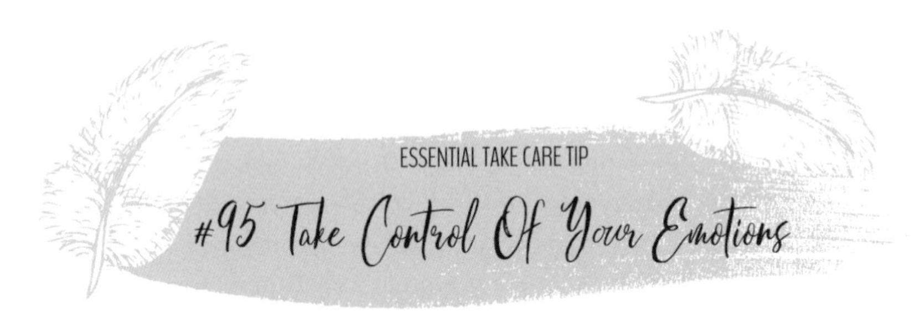

ESSENTIAL TAKE CARE TIP

#95 Take Control Of Your Emotions

Have you ever been having an amazing day, and then one negative thought came in and totally took you down?

It can feel easy to get sucked into a vortex of negative thought patterns and hard to imagine how you're ever going to get out, but remember: a human being has an average of 60,000 thoughts every day...they're not all going to be winners! There are simple steps we can take to manage our mental and emotional states.

This tip comes to us from my friend, Dr. Zia Nix. For the last 25 years, Dr. Zia has been a leader in the Women's Health & Wellness Movement as a licensed chiropractor. She has served thousands of patients, delivering over half a million chiropractic adjustments.

Dr. Zia is a medicine woman. She has personally healed herself after suffering from a series of health crises. Since 1998 she has traveled to over 30 countries to research & study all forms of integrative medicine including chi gong, Essential Oils, energy medicine, emotional intuitive clearings and plant medicine. She is also a Tai Chi Champion who has won 5 gold medals across the globe, from China to New York City.

"The key to shifting emotional state is to honor our emotions and our experiences, without wallowing in them. I like to think of my emotions as toddlers. I'm certainly going to treat them with respect and validate their thoughts and opinions...but I'm not going to let them be the boss of me! Similarly, my emotions get to feel seen, heard, and important -- without letting them control me, " she says.

How does she shift from attachments to negative thoughts? "First, I makes sure everything I'm feeling is actually mine to feel, " Dr. Zia says. "Humans are naturally empathic beings, which means that we can sometimes unknowingly take on the thoughts and feelings of those around us. I swipe Tea Tree in my elbow creases and down my spine to clear any burdens I may be carrying that aren't actually mine to bear. This alone can feel like lifting a massive weight off your shoulders!"

Next, she says, she rubs a drop of Frankincense on her third eye (middle of forehead, slightly above the eyebrows), and crown, which she says allows her to see through the veil of negativity into the truth of the situation. "One of the beliefs that guide my life is that nothing happens to us. Everything happens for us! EVERYTHING! And there is a gift in every experience if we are willing to explore what that gift might be. I know sometimes it's hard to feel and see that clearly, which is where the power of Frankincense comes in."

Dr. Zia says the most important thing to understand when you're feeling really stuck in a difficult state is that "this too shall pass". To help herself get through to the other side, she turns on her diffuser with a blend that awakens other possibilities in her psyche. Citrus oils unlock the creative centers in our brains and help reconnect us to our joy, our childlike nature, and our raw desire.

DR. ZIA NIX'S NEW POSSIBILITIES DIFFUSER BLEND

Ingredients

- 3 Green Mandarin Essential Oil
- 2 Wild Orange Essential Oil
- 2 Tangerine Essential Oil
- 2 Frankincense Essential Oil
- 1 Bergamot Essential Oil
- 1 Grapefruit Essential Oil
- 1 Lime Essential Oil

Method

Following the manufacturer's instructions for your diffuser, add the Oils and water. Then Dr. Zia says...take a few deep breaths, turn on some music, and dance! Changing your physical state has a profoundly positive impact on your thoughts and feelings. Plus, you get to celebrate yourself for taking concrete steps to shift your state!

Bonus...if someone else in your house is suffering from some stinkin' thinkin', the diffuser will help shift them, too!

The biggest mistakes can lead to the greatest successes. How does that work? Don't think of a mistake as a failure; think of it as an opportunity to learn.

When you slip up, it's normal to be upset, and maybe a little mad at yourself. Don't stew about it forever though. Think it over, talk about it with friends or family if you want. Figure out how you could have avoided the mistake or how you will avoid the mistake in the future, and then let it go. And guess what – the mistake that had you feeling so bad now makes you smarter and stronger. Turn the negative feeling into a positive experience and part of your growth.

Stay on track by knowing that there will be times when you will feel sad or worried. Accept that, and know that it's normal. The key is to make sure you don't ignore those kinds of feelings, or blame yourself for having them as you work through them. The goal is not to be perfect, it's to keep moving forward.

BACK IN THE SADDLE DIFFUSER BLEND

Ingredients

3 **Grapefruit Essential Oil**
the sparkling scent helps with clarity, and is a known stress-buster

3 **Lime Essential Oil**
promotes healthy energy flow throughout the body, and helps you re-focus

2 **Peppermint Essential Oil**
provides a powerful physical and mental energy boost

Method

Following the instructions that came with your diffuser, fill it with water. Add the Oils, and enjoy.

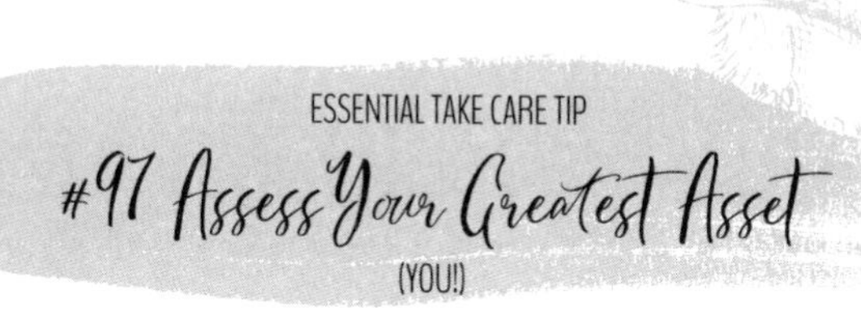

ESSENTIAL TAKE CARE TIP

#97 Assess Your Greatest Asset

(YOU!)

What we're talking about in this chapter, and truly throughout this entire book comes down to the idea of investing in yourself. To do that, you have to believe that you are worth the time and effort---and not just once in a while, every day.

My friend Tiffany Peterson is a Life Coach and a Sales Coach who teaches people about the importance of Self-Care, right along with Sales Training for success. "The relationship you have with yourself influences everything else in your life. Your mindset, your energy, your joy and fulfillment—it all impacts everything and everyone else in your life," she says.

Tiffany teaches that self-trust is the key to manifesting your next biggest dreams and goals. She says your mind, heart, body, and spirit should be your top priorities. How are you doing in those areas? Tiffany offers this exercise in her Self-Care Guide:

1. In your journal, write the headings "Mind", "Heart", "Body", and "Spirit".

2. On a scale of 1-10, how well are you doing taking care of yourself in each of those areas?

3. Now, what one thing could you do to move a notch up that scale? Give those things some energy.

"Everything is energy. Invest in yours. When you feel better, you perform better. I believe that self-trust is the key to manifesting your next biggest dreams and goals" Tiffany says.

WHAT ARE TIFFANY'S GO-TO OILS FOR SELF-CARE?

"Do I have to pick just one?" she says. She loves to use a citrus blend, Rose, Magnolia, and Geranium Oil. Tiffany says she draws a heart on her chest with Rose, then swipes it behind her ears, neck, and wrists. She layers Magnolia behind her ears and neck, and diffuses the citrus blend and Geranium, or makes a rollerball bottle blend with it.

Stress can be a block to positive thinking, and all the health benefits we get from having a positive mindset. We talked a lot in Chapter One about how to reduce and manage daily stress. It's important to bring it up again in this Chapter, because getting a handle on our stress levels clears the way for more optimism. Here's a blend you can make in a roller ball bottle for on-the-go Stress-Less support:

STRESS LESS BLEND

Ingredients

- 1 Vetiver Essential Oil
- 1 Lavender Essential Oil
- 3 Grounding Blend
- 1 Frankincense Essential Oil
- 1 Siberian Fir Essential Oil
- 10 ml Rollerball Bottle
- Fractionated Cocnut Oil

Method

Place drops of Essential Oil into a 10 ml roller bottle and top with Fractionated Coconut Oil. Roll onto wrists, back of neck and behind ears to reduce anxious feelings, tension and nervousness.

We have a link to Tiffany's website in the Resource Guide at the end of this book. You can download her free Self-Care Guide and find a link to her Self-Care = Success video series there, and through www.TakeCareTips.com.

The ancient Greeks believed that self-care was a way to make people more honest citizens who would care for others. The more you love yourself, the more you could love others. Aristotle said, "all friendly feelings for others are an extension of man's feelings for himself."

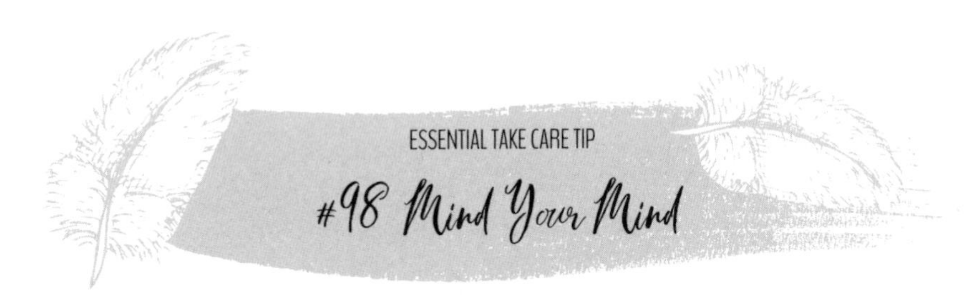

ESSENTIAL TAKE CARE TIP

#98 Mind Your Mind

When we don't take care of our bodies, people can tell! When we don't take care of our minds, it can be harder, and take much longer to spot. My beautiful new friend, Miss United States 2018, Andromeda Peters, is a licensed psychotherapist specializing in mindfulness and utilizes her very own self- love curriculum. She is dedicated to helping address the mental health care crisis in America through her platform of mental health and mindfulness. Besides working with patients in a hospital, she runs Mindful Self-Care workshops for women where she provides them with mental health resources and safety tips so that they can feel supported and powerful. Andromeda also works with a program called Your Mind Matters, where she teaches children in school about the importance of mental health and self-care. Andromeda says we need to focus on taking care of our minds just like we take care of our bodies, and created this acronym to help people remember her mental health wellness tips:

SAM

S is for SUPPORT. Andromeda says don't be afraid to reach out for help. Contact a therapist, join a support group, talk to friends…any core group of people who have your best interest in mind.

A is for AROMATHERAPY. Andromeda is a big believer in the power of scent for mental health. She loves to diffuse Essential Oils to create a positive environment, and she uses them regularly for self-care. In fact, she used two pre-made rollerball blends - one was an Encouraging Blend of citrus and mint Essential Oils, the other was an Inspiring Blend - made up of spicy, floral Essential Oils, for calming during the Miss United States pageant, rolling the Oil on her wrists and smelling it!

M is for MINDFULNESS. "It's important to give your mind a quiet space," Andromeda says. "It races around like we do." She likes to use guided meditation to give her brain some time to relax. She also teaches the benefits of focused breathing: breath in for 4 counts, hold for 4 counts, exhale for 4 counts.

ESSENTIAL TAKE CARE TIP

#99 Aromatic Dressing For Positive Protection

Start your day with the power of positive vision to keep your spirits up. My friend Hanna Keeley, mom of seven (!) TV (and real life) personality, and author of Total Mom Makeover, shared this tip with me. She says, "When you get dressed in the morning, imagine that you are clothing yourself in a shield of joy. Things won't always go as you want them to during the day. Frustrating events and irritating people can try to make you upset but imagine all that negative energy simply rolling off your shield. Don't give anyone or anything the power to rob you of your joy. It's yours to keep."

Another way to clothe yourself in positive energy for the day is through an Essential Oil technique called 'Aromatic Dressing' created by Vanessa Jean Boscarello Ovens. It's a self-care ritual that dresses you in Essential Oils to support overall wellness. Many people who use this technique include affirmations as they use the Oils to help anchor messages of love, acceptance and gratitude.

Vanessa Jean is a top wellness leader and trailblazer in Australia. She's skilled in raw and wholefood cooking for health. Vanessa Jean also has a background in psychology, along with more than twenty years working with aromatherapy. Her passions lie in addressing the emotional and spiritual gifts of the essential oils. She invites people to tune into their daily intentions and create an aligning blend to support themselves. All you need is a few minutes every morning and every evening!

To begin your day renewed, protected and aligned, try Aromatic Dressing…

For Aromatic Dressing, Vanessa Jean mixes her Oils in a small bowl and then dips her fingers in the Oils, rubs her palms together, and beginning from the bottom of her legs, she massages in big circular motions working her way up to her heart.

This is not a slow, light massage. She moves fluidly, and while she dips and rubs, Vanessa Jean acknowledges body parts with positive affirmations of gratitude... "I love you legs, thank you for carrying me day to day," for example.

She says the motion supports the lymphatic system, which has no pump of its own. It also calms the mind and soothes the spirit. Vanessa Jean finishes by massaging Oils on her face, ends of hair, and soles of feet. Then she cups her hands and breathes the Oils in three times, repeating a positive affirmation of love. Visit me at www.takecaretips.com to see Vanessa Jean demonstrate Aromatic Dressing.

You can customize the experience based on what you need---think about and feel into using Oils that best support your intentions - for example, delivering an energy boost in the morning, and calming Oils for bedtime.

Vanessa Jean's Signature Blend features Frankincense, Lavender and Wild Orange. It smells wonderful. She recommends using this for her Aromatic Dressing self-love ritual. Try it to change your outlook!

VANESSA JEAN'S SIGNATURE BLEND

Ingredients

- 2 Frankincense Essential Oil
- 2 Wild Orange Essential Oil
- 1 Lavender Essential Oil
- 10 ml Fractionated Coconut Oil
- 10 ml Rollerball Bottle (optional)

Method

Add each Oil to a small bowl when you're ready to use them for Aromatic Dressing. You can also use this as a diffuser blend (minus the Fractionated Coconut Oil), or use the recipe as is, adding everything to a rollerball bottle to wear as a "purefume" and keep that happy energy going throughout your day. Regarding the ratios, Vanessa Jean recommends a total of 5 drops in 10 ml for adults, 2-3 drops in 10ml carrier oil for children, and 1-2 drops in 10 ml carrier oil for babies.

ESSENTIAL TAKE CARE TIP

#100 Forgive

The anger and guilt that we carry around with us weighs us down. That heaviness can make us bitter, and actually hurt us physically as well as emotionally (like we learned in Chapter Two). Cut those chains by allowing yourself to forgive. Whether it's resentment toward another person, or something you've done that you deeply regret, try to think of forgiveness as something that will help you grow.

It's also good to note that forgiving something doesn't mean you approve of the behavior that hurt you. You don't have to approve of it to reach a place where you can move past it. Forgiveness is an internal process. Give yourself the grace you need to move through it. To start the process, take ten minutes to journal about what forgiveness means to you, and how you will feel with that heaviness is lifted.

There are Essential Oils that can support you as you work at forgiveness. Try this beautiful diffuser blend:

RELEASE DIFFUSER BLEND

Ingredients

5 Lemon Essential Oil
cleans away negative feelings

3 Cardamom Essential Oil
supports respiratory function. Take a deep breath and move on

Method

Following the instructions that came with your diffuser, fill it with water. Add the Oils, and enjoy.

ESSENTIAL TAKE CARE TIP

#101 Say A Little Prayer

I've heard from many that one of the most powerful experiences they have while caring for a sick loved one is praying with them.

You can find comfort and strength in simple words like, "Lord, let me feel your love." Repeating those few words can help you feel more connected, calm, and secure. Allow yourself ten minutes of quiet time and just speak from the heart.

A PRAYER FOR YOU

Here is a blessing for you written by a Bishop David Zubik, who was also a caregiver for his parents. Again, no matter what your spiritual beliefs, finding a way to have faith that you are not alone, that a force more powerful than you is able to help you and guide you, can add great positive energy to your life.

Dear Father in Heaven,

We ask you to bless the caregivers
who tend to the sick,
the infirm,
the elderly,
and the children,
all those who cannot care for themselves.

We pray that you especially bless
those who are caring for family members.

Help all the caregivers to be strong,
patient, and tender in their mininstry.

Lift up their spirits, Lord,
that they may find gladness in their work
and share your joy and peace
with those in their care.

May the healing power of the Holy Spirit
refresh them in mind and body.

Lighten their burdens,
and prepare all of us for that day
when we shall joyfully meet the Great Healer,
your Son, Jesus Christ. AMEN.

A FINAL THOUGHT FROM ME TO YOU...

My hope and prayer for you is that you will make the time to nurture the strength you need to make caring for yourself a priority. You are giving so much of yourself, and making lives better as a result. Find the time to reflect on how special that is. Allow yourself to feel pride. Make positive changes to manage the caregiver part of your life, and do everything you can to keep the other important parts of your life alive. Rejoice for the time that you have with your loved ones, and for the opportunities you have to be with them to experience life's challenges and blessings.

I hope this isn't goodbye for us. Please keep this book on your shelf and come back to it when you need a little boost in a particular area. Share it with others who become caregivers.

I'd love to continue the conversation with you – join me at www.TakeCareTips.com.

Take care!

With love

j.

The burdens of caregiving scream, the blessings whisper. Take care of yourself to keep an open heart and mind that allow you to hear those whispers."

–Jennifer Antkowiak

Resource guide

For more Essential Take Care Tips, information about caregiving, healthy living, and some wonderful tools for a happy you, please visit me at
www.TakeCareTips.com.

For Essential Oil supplies and healthy living products
www.YourOilTools.com (USA)
www.eosupplies.com (Europe)

There's a wealth of caregiving information and support online. Here are some excellent places to start:

The National Family Caregivers Association at
www.NFCACares.org

The National Alliance for Caregiving at
www.Caregiving.org

The National Caregivers Library at
www.CaregiversLibrary.org

Online magazine Today's Caregiver at
www.Caregiving.com

American Association of Retired Persons (AARP) Caregiver support at
www.AARP.org/family/caregiving

Online caregiving resource site
www.Caring.com

For information on heart health, visit the American Heart Association at
www.AmericanHeart.org

For mind/body balance and stress-relief, information and products, visit Health Psychologist Dr. Nancy Mramor's website. Find some of Dr. Mramor's techniques in Essential Take Care Tip #3 (Better Breathing) and Essential Take Care Tip #11 (Balance Your Brain).
www.realconsciousliving.com

For more information about healthy hormone solution, and healthy living, visit Dr. Mariza Snyder's website. Find an oil blend from Dr. Mariza in essential take care tip #73 (Mission control). www.drmariza.com

For information on walking your way to health, visit fitness expert Leslie Sansone's website. Walk at Home is the #1 in-home walking program in the world. Learn about Leslie's 10-min walking workout in Essential Take Care Tip #22 (Just Walk).
www.WalkAtHome.com
www.Walk15.com

For information on the Food Pyramid and the USDA's dietary guidelines.
www.MyPyramid.gov.

For information on sleep and sleep disorders, visit the National Sleep Foundation .
www.SleepFoundation.org.

To stop junk mail, and other solicitations, as featured in Essential Tip #71 (Get Off The List), visit the following websites:
www.DMAChoice.org
www.OptOutPreScreen.com

For information on simplifying and managing life, home and business, including sales training, visit author Mj Callaway. Find an idea from Mj in Essential take care tip #72 (clear your desk)
www.MjCallaway.com

For information on organizing and de-cluttering your life, visit organization and motivation expert Meryl Starr. Find an idea from Meryl in Essential Take Care Tip #75 (Color Coded Closet).
www.MerylStarr.com

For parenting and healthy living information, visit Hannah Keeley, author of Total Mom Makeover. Find an idea from Hannah in Essential Take Care Tip #99 (Aromatic Dressing for Positive Protection).
www.HannahKeeley.com

For coaching to create a life and business you love, visit Tiffany Peterson's website. Find an idea from Tiffany in Essential Take Care Tip #97 (Assess Your Greatest Asset).
www.tiffanyspeaks.com

For more information about supporting a healthy mind, visit Miss United States Andromeda Peters. Find an idea from Andromeda in Essential Take Care Tip #98 (Mind Your Mind).
Instagram: @andromedapeters,
& @selflovetherapist.

For more information about healthy lifestyle, visit Jackie Ritz at her website. Find a an idea from Jackie in Essential Take Care Tip #42 (Bone Broth).
www.ThePaleoMama.com

For information about natural healing with Chinese Medicine, Essential Oils, and energy work, visit Desiree Mangandog.
www.DesireeMangandog.com

For more information about bestselling cookbook author and recipe developer Tenina Holder, visit Tenina's website. Tenina's delicious recipes are featured in Essential Take Care Tip #16 (Raspberry and Wild Orange Ganache Truffles), Tip #34 (Honey and Mustard butter glaze) and Tip #37 (Haloumi and Watermelon Salad)
www.Tenina.com

For more information on healthy living and using food as medicine, visit Vanessa Jean's website. Find an idea from Vanessa Jean in Essential Take Care Tip #99 (Aromatic Dressing for Positive Protection)
www.foodalchemy.com.au.

Acknowledgments

The messages in this book come from my heart. I am happy for the opportunity to acknowledge and show my gratitude to those who helped them flow out in Essential Take Care Tips:

My mother and mother-in-law, who put me on this path and fuel my passion to help others. I feel their heavenly hugs always. My dad, who encouraged my desire to become an author at age six, and hand-stitched my very first book. He's taught me that we each have all the strength we need. My grandmothers – for their love and guidance. Becky, Jessie, and Katy – for wrapping their big sister in positive thoughts and for keeping family a priority. Pap, who brought so much to our lives. My beautiful step-daughter, Bethany, for her love. My sweet Michael, Alexander, Nicholas, Grace, and Joseph – who make me feel like the luckiest Mum in the world every day; just writing their names makes my heart happy. My husband Joe for his undying belief in me, which helps me to believe in myself.

The St. Lynn's Press team, who I worked with on the original version of this book; and my new creative and publishing family---I'm so grateful for their emotional investment in this message. We worked together through various time zones to complete this beautiful project: Steve Kesselring and his team at Your Oil Tools. Vivien Garside from Essential Oil Supplies Ltd for working closely with me in bringing the book to life, creating such a beautiful design (with her talented team of designers) and editing the content with me. I'm so excited for more good things ahead to compliment Essential Take Care Tips!

Every person I interviewed for the book, for the gift of their time to talk with me and share information in an effort to help others. My friend, photographer Becky Thurner, who gave her time and talent to capture images to convey the positive feelings and energy we want to send out to caregivers. Fr. John Skirtich for his blessings on this book, and our mission to help caregivers. My dear friend and business mentor Leslie Sansone for starting me on a walk to a new and exciting journey, and for not ever leaving me alone for too long on this path. My friends and neighbors who cheered this project on.

And God for…well…everything.

How should I get started with Essential Oils?

Let's have a look at the Top 10 Essential Oils you will want to welcome into your life, because of their versatility. Used individually, and in combinations, these Oils provide physical, emotional, environmental and spiritual support.

Here's a very brief introduction to the rockstars I recommend for you to get into your home ASAP!

---

1. **LEMON:** Lemon Essential Oil cleanses the body and supports healthy digestion, a positive mood, and healthy respiratory function. It's also wonderful to use in DIY non-toxic cleaning products.

2. **LAVENDER:** Lavender Essential Oil is all things calming. It helps to calm the body and mind, and supports relaxation and better quality sleep. It is also great to have on hand to soothe skin irritations, include insect bites and burns.

3. **PEPPERMINT:** Peppermint Essential Oil provides a natural energy boost. It's cooling to the skin, and supports a healthy digestive and respiratory system.

4. **TEA TREE:** Tea Tree Essential Oil is known as "First Aid for the Skin". It can be used to help a variety of skin conditions, as well as after minor scrapes and scratches. Tea Tree is also good for healthy fingernails and toenails, and can be added to shampoo to support a healthy scalp.

5. **OREGANO:** Oregano Essential Oil is known as "Nature's Antibiotic" and provides potent immune support. Dilute a drop or less in Fractionated Coconut Oil and apply to skin, or nails to help with viral, fungal, and bacterial infections. Oregano is also used in DIY cleaning solutions for mold and mildew.

6. **FRANKINCENSE:** Frankincense is known as "The King of Oils", and is used for brain support, and cellular function. It is also considered a powerful anti-inflammatory, and supports a healthy immune system and nervous system. Frankincense Essential can be mixed with Fractionated Coconut Oil as an anti-aging serum for the face and neck. People also love to use Frankincense during meditation.

7. **THE PROTECTIVE BLEND:** The Protective Blend is a heavy-duty mixture of Wild Orange, Clove, Cinnamon, Eucalyptus, and Rosemary Essential Oils that can be used for immune support, diffused to neutralize airborne pathogens, and as a mouthwash. The Protective Blend also makes an effective, and inexpensive household cleaning spray.

8. **THE RESPIRATORY BLEND:** The Respiratory Blend is a mixture of Laurel Leaf, Eucalyptus, Peppermint, Tea Tree, Lemon, Cardamom, Ravintsara, and Ravensara Essential Oils, and is used to support healthy breathing. This is a popular blend to use at the change of seasons, and in a diffuser to help with a better night's sleep.

9. **THE DIGESTIVE BLEND:** The Digestive Blend features Essential Oils known to soothe the digestive tract: Anise, Peppermint, Ginger, Caraway, Corriander, Tarragon, and Fennel. Just a drop diluted with Fractionated Coconut Oil massaged into the belly, along the spine, the soles of the feet, or across the chest helps with a variety of symptoms related to an upset stomach.

10. **THE SOOTHING BLEND:** The Soothing Blend is made up of Wintergreen, Camphor, Peppermint, Ylang Ylang, Helichrysum, Blue Tansy, Roman Chamomile, and Osmanthus Essential Oils. This is the go-to blend to soothe sore, tired, muscles and joints.

Would you like to learn more? Please visit me at www.TakeCareTips.com. I have additional information and support for you there. You can also order these Oils (and others) in the Shop.

ABOUT THE AUTHOR

Jennifer Antkowiak is a top Wellness Educator, and natural solutions provider; as well as a self-care author, and keynote speaker, with honors and awards for leadership. She had a 25-year career as a trusted, beloved, award-winning TV news anchor and reporter, most of which was spent at KDKA-TV (CBS-Pittsburgh) sharing stories that impacted people's lives. Audiences say they love her warmth, wit, and wisdom; which comes through in her talks and teachings.

Jen also serves as an adjunct professor, teaching business and communications courses at a private college in Pennsylvania.

For more than a decade, she's been a sought after coach and consultant, helping corporations support caregivers in the workplace. Her Take Care Tips presentations provide continuing education for nurses, social workers, and nursing home and hospice administrators.

Jen is a nationally certified fitness instructor, and is the Director of Walk 15 (www.Walk15.com), a group fitness program that licenses Walk 15 Instructors to teach classes all around the world.

She is blessed to be a wife and mum to five children plus a step-daughter. She'd tell you they bring an enormous amount of light and love to her life.

Jen is passionate about empowering others to take better care of themselves, and invited you to connect with her through her website, www.TakeCareTips.com for more tips and self-care strategies.